"Tracing shining ways through fiord and sound, past forests and waterfalls, islands and mountains, and far azure headlands, it seems as if surely we must at length reach the very paradise of the poets, the abode of the blessed."

- John Muir, Travels in Alaska

A favorite from my collection of historic Alaska photographs is this scene from Port Clarence, near the Arctic Circle, around 1880. In the distance are seven steam whalers (two are behind the tent on the left) and two smaller schooners, the latter probably used for trading. You can clearly see six of the protected barrel-like crow's nests on the masts of the whalers.

In the foreground are two canvas tents next to a kayak, its hull made of caribou or seal skin stretched over a drift-wood frame. Standing on the left-hand tent frame are what appear to be hoops of seal skin or perhaps whale blubber drying. On the post are some carved ivory figures.

There are few protected harbors in northwest Alaska, and this one on the Seward Peninsula not far from Nome was a favorite anchorage for whalers. UW NA2125

Part of this book appeared in the previous edition, titled The Alaska Cruise Explorer
2018 Edition

Coastal Publishing
P.O. Box 110, Vinalhaven, ME 04863
Printed in Canada

Maps by Joe Upton

Photographs by Joe Upton unless noted with the following abbreviations:
AMNH - American Museum of Natural History, New York
AM - Anchorage Museum
AS - AlaskaStock
BCARS - British Columbia Archives and Records Service
BCRM- British Columbia Royal Museum
CRMM - Columbia River Maritime Museum, Astoria, Oregon
DK - Dan Kowalski
MOHAI - Museum of History and Industry, Seattle
SFM - San Francisco Maritime Museum
THS - Tongass Historical Society, Ketchikan, Alaska
UAF - University of Alaska, Fairbanks
UW - University of Washington Special Collections
WAT - Whatcom County (WA) Museum of History and Art

ISBN 978-0-9887981-8-2

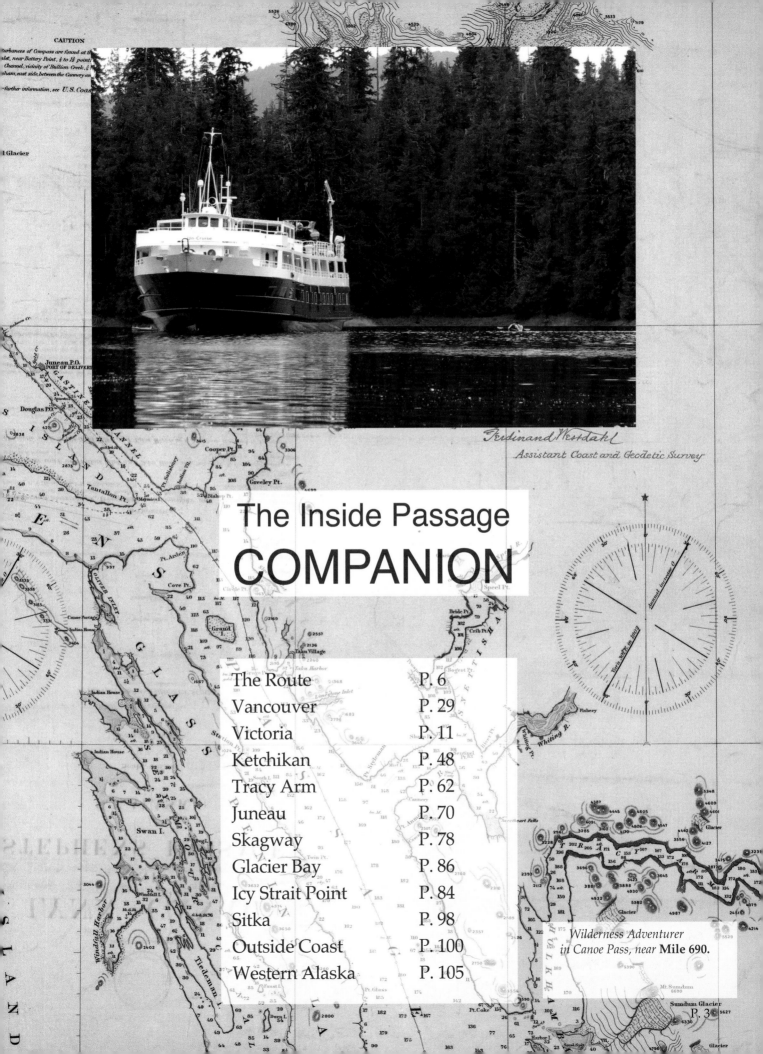

Ferdinand Westdahl
Assistant Coast and Geodetic Survey

The Inside Passage
COMPANION

*Wilderness Adventurer
in Canoe Pass, near* **Mile 690.**

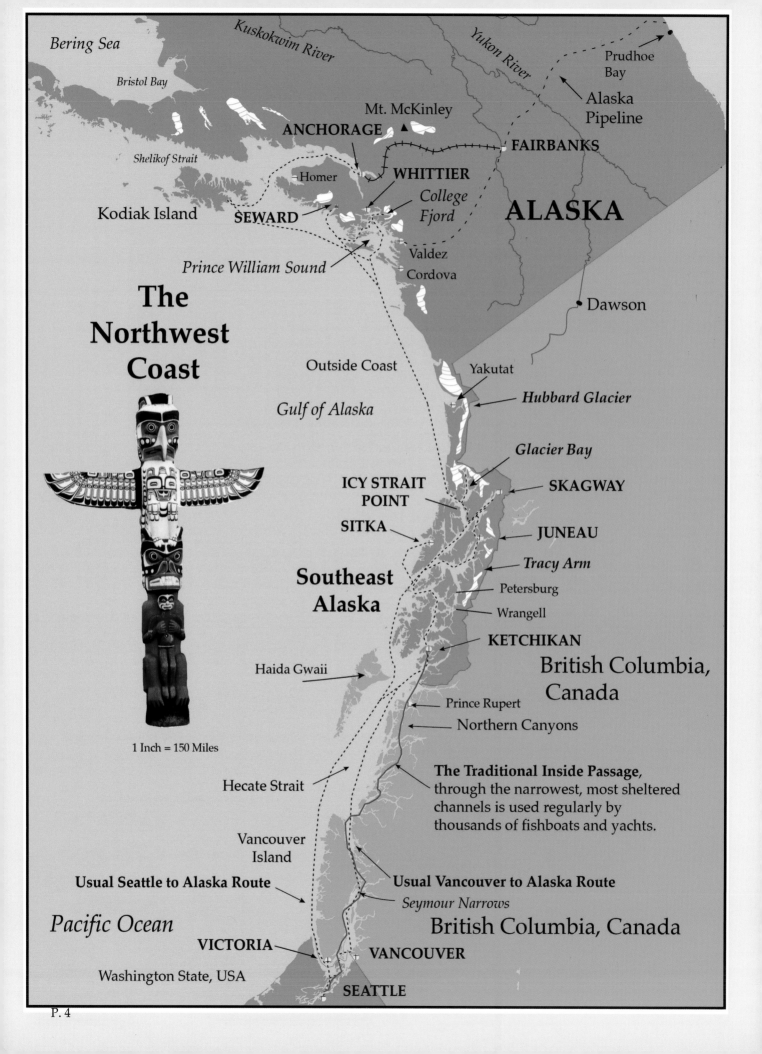

Bering Sea

Bristol Bay

Kuskokwim River

Yukon River

Prudhoe Bay

Alaska Pipeline

Shelikof Strait

Mt. McKinley

ANCHORAGE

FAIRBANKS

Homer

WHITTIER

College Fjord

ALASKA

Kodiak Island

SEWARD

Valdez

Cordova

Prince William Sound

Dawson

The Northwest Coast

Outside Coast

Yakutat

Gulf of Alaska

Hubbard Glacier

Glacier Bay

ICY STRAIT POINT

SKAGWAY

SITKA

JUNEAU

Southeast Alaska

Tracy Arm

Petersburg

Wrangell

KETCHIKAN

British Columbia, Canada

Haida Gwaii

1 Inch = 150 Miles

Prince Rupert

Northern Canyons

Hecate Strait

The Traditional Inside Passage, through the narrowest, most sheltered channels is used regularly by thousands of fishboats and yachts.

Vancouver Island

Usual Seattle to Alaska Route

Usual Vancouver to Alaska Route

Seymour Narrows

Pacific Ocean

British Columbia, Canada

VICTORIA

VANCOUVER

Washington State, USA

SEATTLE

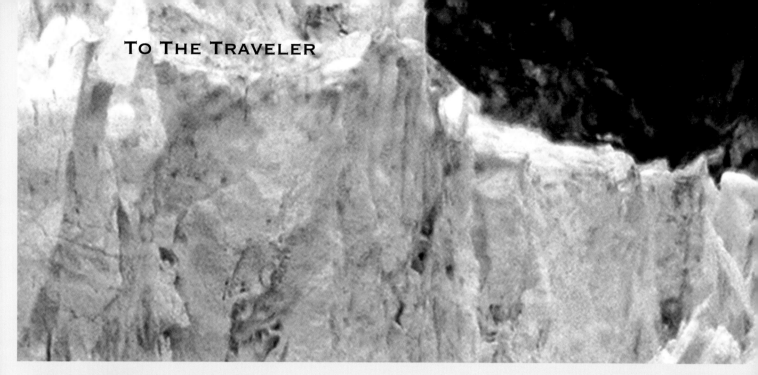

Mickey Hansen and me, Southeast Alaska, 1965. He showed me the ways of The North and filled my head with wonderful stories.

Mile 30

Look for these video icons *in this book and on our maps. They refer to our 3-5 minute mini-documentary videos that we have created at specific places along the Inside Passage. They may be seen on the video page of www. joeupton.com.*

Our map and navigation system: *this book is designed to be used in conjunction with our illustrated* **Alaska Cruise Map***, available on Amazon and on many ships. Ship routes are shown with numbers based on a "Seattle is Mile Zero," system. Many ships use this system to announce ship position, such as "We are now at mile 522 on your map."*

When I was a green kid of 18, I had a powerful experience—working my first Alaska job on a fish-buying boat, delivering salmon to a remote Native-owned cannery. Mickey Hansen, the grizzled Norwegian mate who had worked 50 seasons "up North," took me under his wing and shared with me the lore and legends of this vast region. That kindly old man was full of wonderful stories: "We went in there in the old *Mary A*, winter of '31. Thick o' snow, we'd toot that horn and listen for the echo off the rocks, through the snow." In this way, he gave me a passion for The North that I still have to this day.

For twenty years, I worked the coast in all kinds of boats, in all kinds of weather. I was a fish-buyer, a salmon fisherman, a king crab fisherman decades before "The Deadliest Catch."

When the wind blew, the anchor would go down and the rum bottle and the stories would come out.

When the big cruise ships started coming north, I designed a series of books with illustrated maps to share with these new visitors the drama and beauty of The North.

A few years ago, I started working with commercial fisherman/filmmaker Dan Kowalski. We'd take his boat to remote places and film short stories about what had happened there.

For me, the books and maps at first, and later the videos, were a way to share a sense of the mystery and the power of this place that is such a big part of my life.

So, come take this journey through a land that remains much as it was when the first explorers came through.

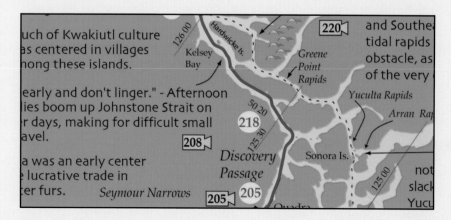

uch of Kwakiutl culture as centered in villages nong these islands.

early and don't linger." - Afternoon ies boom up Johnstone Strait on r days, making for difficult small avel.

a was an early center e lucrative trade in er furs.

Seymour Narrows

Kelsey Bay

Hardwicke Is.

Greene Point Rapids

220

and Southe tidal rapids obstacle, as of the very

Yuculta Rapids

Arran Ra

208

218

Discovery Passage

Sonora Is.

not slack Yucu

205 205

Quadra

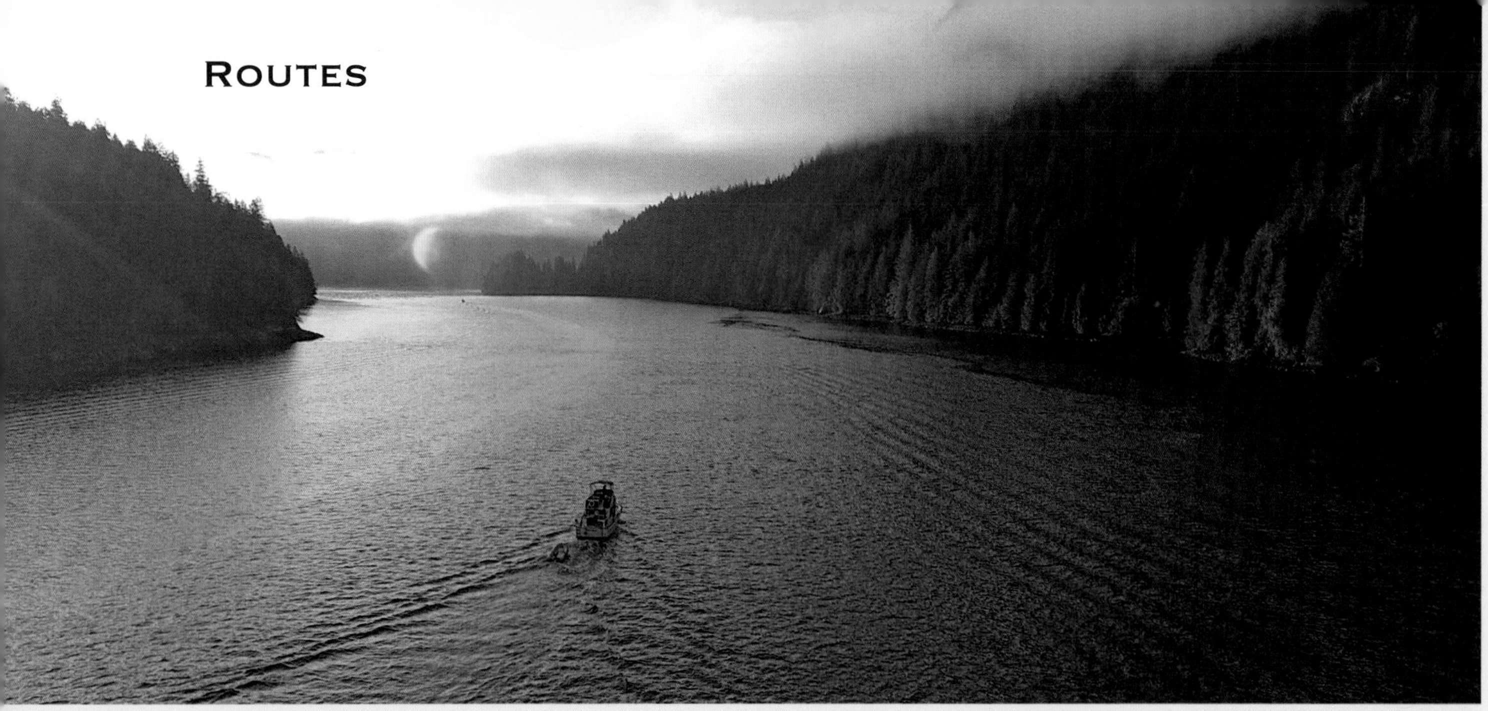

The Inside Passage is the collective name for a series of winding channels and waterways, wide and narrow, that allow even very small craft, to travel to Alaska in relative safety.

At a number of places - Juan de Fuca Strait, Georgia Strait, Johnstone Strait, Queen Charlotte Sound, Milbank Sound, and Dixon Entrance, the crossings are exposed enough that prudence dictates that the mariner listen carefully to weather reports. But by doing so, and making sure not to travel through areas where the wind and a strong tidal flow are opposed to each other, even kayakers and rowboats have made it all the way to Alaska.

The smaller a craft is, the more protected channel it will prefer. The traditional route is the one outlined in Captain Farwell's **Hansen Handbook**, a listing of point to point courses that allowed mariners to travel to Alaska without having to buy a stack of charts or expensive chartbooks. However in numerous places, particularly through the Discovery Islands, there are numerous even narrower and more winding routes, like the one above.

It's about 650 miles from Seattle to Ketchikan, Alaska, a journey that would take a typical fishing boat or small yacht, traveling at 8-10 mph, a week or longer. Vessels this size typically only travel daylight hours so as to be able to see logs in the water, and anchoring up each night.

Once a vessel leaves the busy Georgia Strait area around **Mile 205**, the trip north is essentially through wilderness.

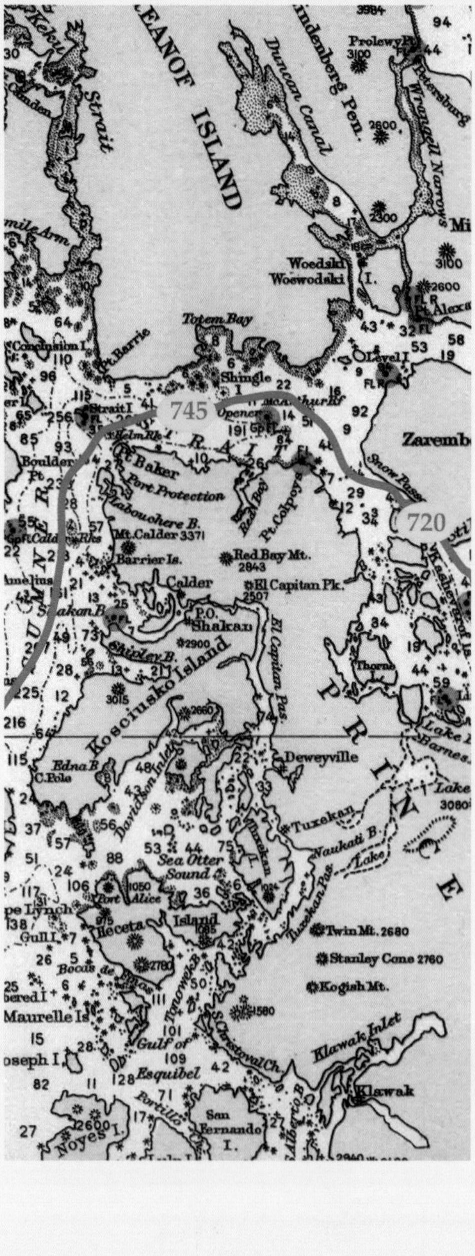

Top: In Cordero Channel, just north of Yuculta Rapids, **Mile 212 E.** *Right: Sumner Strait, Alaska, showing cruise route between Ketchikan and Juneau. Bottom: section of* **Hansen Handbook** *(see above.)*

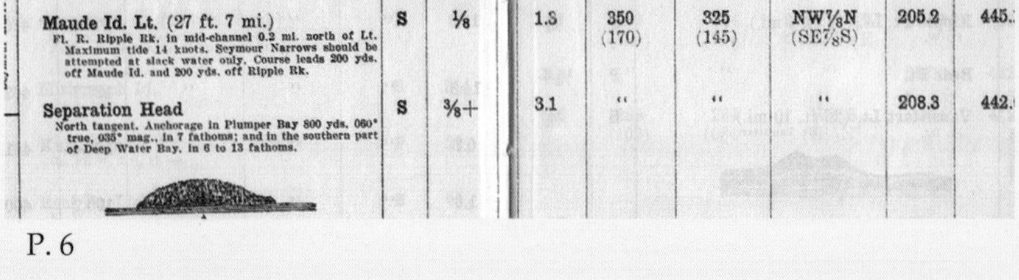

Seattle to Ketchikan Via Active Pass and Inside	Port or Stbd. Beam	Dist. off Miles	Distance Pt. to Pt.	True Course	Magnetic Course	Magnetic in Points	Distance From Point of Departure	Distanc to Des-tinatio
			(Reverse Courses in Parentheses)					
Steep Id. Change on highest pt. To anchor in Duncan Bay, round to 263° true, 238° mag., putting north end Steep Id. astern; run 0.7 mi. past Orange Pt. abeam and anchor ⅜ mi. off shore, in 13 fathoms. Head on east side Maude Id.	S	⅜	1.6	319 (139)	294 (114)	NWxW⅞W (SExE⅞E)	200.7	449.
Race Pt. Lt. (70 ft. 14 mi.) Fl. G. Heavy tide rips when flooding. Round at this distance.	P	⅜	3.2	296 (116)	271 (091)	W⅛N (E⅛S)	203.9	446.
Maude Id. Lt. (27 ft. 7 mi.) Fl. R. Ripple Rk. in mid-channel 0.2 mi. north of Lt. Maximum tide 14 knots. Seymour Narrows should be attempted at slack water only. Course leads 200 yds. off Maude Id. and 200 yds. off Ripple Rk.	S	⅛	1.3	350 (170)	325 (145)	NW⅞N (SE⅞S)	205.2	445.
Separation Head North tangent. Anchorage in Plumper Bay 800 yds. 060° true, 035° mag., in 7 fathoms; and in the southern part of Deep Water Bay, in 6 to 13 fathoms.	S	⅜+	3.1	"	"	"	208.3	442.

*Top: View of the Inside Passage, showing Fraser Reach in the vicinity of Khutze and Altanash Inlets, **Mile 468**. Sadly, few ships take this route any more, preferring the slightly shorter but much less interesting route straight up Hecate Strait.*

Above: Captain Turner takes the Volendam *straight up Grenville Channel, about 50 miles north of where the top photo was taken. Bravo Captain Turner: if your Captain takes this route, make sure you let the ship know you appreciate it. Such side trips are less and less common.*

The key word is **inside -** when the Pleistocene glaciers carved their way down the Northwest Coast in the last ice age some 30,000 years ago, they left behind a mariner's paradise. Ten major islands and as many as a thousand smaller ones, rocks, and reefs allowed mariners to chose one of many routes north.

Before about 1897, few vessels ventured much north of Vancouver Island. But after John Muir "discovered" Glacier Bay (actually the Indians knew about the Bay long before he arrived by canoe in 1867) and described it in his powerful style, some steamers would make a few round trips between Seattle and the glaciers each summer.

A couple of lucky prospectors in 1896 changed all that, when they discovered a rich vein of gold near the tiny settlement of Dawson in Canada's remote Yukon Territories. It was so remote that it took almost a year for the word to get out. But when it did, and suddenly tens of thousands of prospectors struck with severe cases of gold fever arrived in Seattle, Vancouver, San Francisco, and Portland, unscrupulous ship owners pressed tired and occasionally seaworthy ships into service to take the hordes to Alaska.

The route they took - inside of Vancouver Island in protected waters, briefly out into rougher waters across the lower end of Hecate Strait, then into the sheltered waters again of Fitzhugh Sound, Lama Passage, Seaforth Channel, Milbanke Sound, Tolmie Channel, Graham Reach, Fraser Reach, and finally the legendary Granville Channel and Chatham Sound to the Alaska border at breezy Dixon Entrance became the traditional Inside Passage.

And once they finally crossed into Alaska at **Mile 600**, they had another 400 plus miles of sheltered waters. For almost all the Gold Rush ships, their final destination was Skagway, 1020 sheltered inside miles from Seattle.

A few very brave paddlewheelers left sheltered waters at **Cape Spencer, Mile 1020** to head up along very unfriendly shores to the north and west, for over **another thousand miles** on to the mouth of the Yukon River. And then almost 2500 miles finally to the diggings at Dawson. Whew!

The big boom in Alaska cruise ships started in the 1980s. At first most ships took the traditional route. But as ships got bigger, they found the narrower passages, like Lama Pass, and especially the tight turn at **Boat Bluff, Mile 439**, too constricted, and eventually gave up this part of the route entirely, electing to travel instead up wide, boring Hecate Strait.

THE MIGHTY EMPIRE OF THE WOODS

When English explorer George Vancouver sailed into Puget Sound in the spring of 1792, he was stunned by its beauty and promise. Today, much of that promise has been fulfilled as the land has filled up with people, homes, and businesses.

First was the lumber business. When the first settlers arrived, little did they know that the just starting California Gold Rush was the beginning of a seemingly insatiable demand for timber that could only be satisfied by the kind of good harbors and vast stands of timber that was the hallmark of Puget Sound. Axes echoed in the woods and steam whistles called the men to work in ports up and down the sheltered waters of the lower Inside Passage, as an industry was created that dominated much of the 20th century, and remains important in the 21st.

Next came manufacturing, primarily aircraft, as Boeing became the largest airplane maker in the world, dominating the employment scene as well as keeping literally hundreds of small fabrication operations busy making parts for the big jets.

Then this college dropout named Bill Gates came up with this language for operating computers and the high tech industry that was to eventually rival aircraft manufacturing, began rolling. Next, this guy Howard Schulz had the crazy idea that he could create worldwide demand for his brand of coffee and the shops that sold it. Another entrepreneur, Jeff Bezos, had this really out there idea of an online store that would sell you almost anything.

Turned out that their ideas weren't that crazy after all, and by the time 2015 rolled around, Microsoft, Amazon, Starbucks, Google, and other high tech companies were on the way to transforming Seattle into the third fastest growing city in the US.

Those who came for work found plenty to like: mild climate, thriving arts and music scene, spectacular scenery and wilderness close at hand. The downside was that the real estate market looked like it might eventually become like Southern California, where half a million bucks would barely buy a starter home.

Mile Zero *of The Inside Passage begins in Seattle at Colman Dock. Look for the big ferries; they carry 2000 passengers and 220 cars from busy downtown Seattle to rural Kitsap County.*

Mile 2 - *Akli Beach... It was here that Seattle's first settlers, slogged ashore in a rainstorm in November, 1851. The women of the party, who'd spent the previous six months struggling with the rigors of the Oregon Trail, broke into tears when they saw the promised land: a roofless cabin at the edge of a gloomy forest.*

Mile 7 - *To the west here is the entrance to the locks which separate the salt water of Puget Sound from a connected series of fresh water lakes. I began my first journey to Alaska in my own commercial fishing boat here on a spring morning in 1972:*

"Today on as fine a Seattle morning as I have seen this year, the mountains pink both to east and west, we slip through the locks and down into the salt water of Puget Sound.

"So it all begins. After months of preparation, we're off to travel almost a thousand miles north to fish for salmon, to make a year's living in just a few months. We've done all that we can to be ready, but still, the season ahead is far from certain."

Top: a proud skipper stands on his deckload of Puget Sound Douglas Fir. F12.21.725M

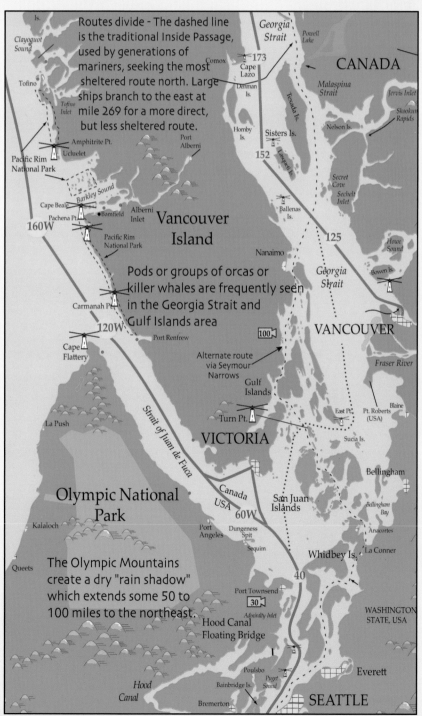

Routes divide - The dashed line is the traditional Inside Passage, used by generations of mariners, seeking the most sheltered route north. Large ships branch to the east at mile 269 for a more direct, but less sheltered route.

Pods or groups of orcas or killer whales are frequently seen in the Georgia Strait and Gulf Islands area

Alternate route via Seymour Narrows

The Olympic Mountains create a dry "rain shadow" which extends some 50 to 100 miles to the northeast.

Mile 14 - *Kingston Ferry, one of the four major routes that take thousands of workers every day to work from homes across Puget Sound.*

Mile 19 - *Possession Point: over the bluff east of here is the Boeing Co., airline builder to the world.*

Mile 25 - *Foulweather Bluff is the entrance to Hood Canal, home to the Pacific nuclear sub fleet and one of many area bridges that sank or blew down in storms. The present Hood Canal bridge was rebuilt after its predecessor sank in a 1979 windstorm.*

Mile 30

Mile 38 - *Port Townsend, with Victorian homes overlooking the water, is a center for arts and crafts and especially the building and care of wooden boats.*

Mile 40 - *Point Wilson is the lighthouse on the point and marks the transition between the calmer waters of Puget Sound and the rougher waters beyond. Three forts were built on the land surrounding this entrance here in the 1890s, creating a "triangle of death," where the intersecting fire from their cannons could sink any enemy ship trying to enter.*

Mile 50W - *Sequim rain shadow: The high ridge of the Olympic Mountains serves to scrape the rain out of the storms sweeping in from the Pacific Ocean, creating a much drier and sunnier climate here.*

Mile 60W: *Orcas are often seen in these waters, particularly along the Vancouver Island shore.*

Mile 80W: *Olympic National Park occupies much of the Olympic Peninsula south of here.*

Mile 90W: *A spot known as "one square inch of silence" is hidden in the Ho Rain Forest south of here. It is believed to be the quietest places in the continental U.S.*

Mile 100W - *Look around; the land on both sides is much wilder here and less and less populated as you approach the outer coast.*

While Vancouver—just 75 miles to the northeast—is a modern, cosmopolitan city with a heavy sprinkling of Asian immigrants, Victoria seems more like a taste of Olde England. Originally settled around a Hudson's Bay Company trading post established in 1843, this city and Vancouver Island became a crown colony in 1849. Ten years later, another colony was established on the mainland to support the many prospectors who had arrived with the 1858 Fraser River gold strike. Eventually the two colonies merged to form what is today British Columbia. Victoria became its capital, while Vancouver became the industrial center.

Victoria is a good place to shop for First Nations (coastal native) art and craft souvenirs. Many shops also specialize in goods from England that are hard to find elsewhere.

Because there are often orca or humpback whales in the vicinity, fast whale watching boats leave regularly from along the waterfront. Twelve miles from downtown Victoria is Butchart Gardens, one of the most popular attractions in the province. This stunning 50-acre showpiece had a rather humble beginning. In 1904, Jennnie Butchart, whose husband operated a nearby cement plant, got tired of staring at the ugly scar that his limestone quarrying operations left. She brought in a few plants to spruce up the area and one thing led to another.

Also downtown across the street to the south from the big Empress Hotel (where the afternoon tea is an elegant ritual), is the excellent British Columbia Provincial Museum. Behind it to the east is an impressive display of totem poles, open around the clock.

Opposite page: The Empress Hotel dominates the Victoria waterfront.
Top: Totem near the Provincial Museum
Left: Statue in Butchart Gardens

THE WILD OUTSIDE COAST

Mile 120W: *Cape Flattery is the northwest corner of the continental U.S. The coast to the south of here is remote and rugged.*

Above: First Beach, just south of the mouth of the Quillayute River, at the Native American village of La Push, WA. Whole trees, sometime four or five feet in diameter, are carried downriver by the current, creating dangers for mariners.

Opposite top: James Island and the entrance to the Quillayute River. In stormy weather, the seas break all the way across the channel, and mariners, desperately seeking shelter, occasionally chance it anyway, risking and occasionally losing their lives.

Opposite lower: even radar didn't keep this tanker safe; all escaped, but the heavy swells made quick work of her hull. Marine Digest photo

In the USA only Alaska and Hawaii have coasts as wild and remote as northwest Washington. Much is total wilderness, the few settlements populated by Native Americans. Only in a very few places can you even get a car to the actual beach. For most, there is only a trail, winding though tall stands of Douglas fir, hemlock, and spruce with thorny devil's club at their base.

The closer you get to the actual shore the wilder it gets, the trees bent and broken by the winter storms. The trail gets steeper, the wind gets stronger. If you are unfamiliar with the tides and arrive when it is high, there might not be any beach at all, just a jumble of huge logs, surging up and down in the seas.

Mariners, approaching these shores before the advent of modern electronics had a name for these waters: The Graveyard of The Pacific. Often wrapped in fog, the full rigged sailing ships and steamers of the day would approach using dead reckoning: estimating their progress from their last position fix - by the stars if coming across the Pacific, often days earlier. The currents conspired against mariners as well, pushing northeast, toward the reef strewn shores.

Often the first indication that they would be off course would be the roar of the breakers just before they hit the rocks.

Greek Tanker, 1969. A week later only small pieces were left.

" April 29, 1792. At four o'clock [a.m.] a sail was discovered to the westward standing in shore. This was a very great novelty, not having seen any vessel but our consort, during the last eight months."

THE EXPLORER

Mile 120W to Mile 158W - *the old Shipwreck Trail along the coast of British Columbia. So many ships piled up on the rocks here that a trail was built, with huts at intervals stocked with food and firewood and a telephone to the nearest lighthouse. Many a mariner staggered into these cabins, ever so grateful to whoever built and stocked them. Now popular with hikers seeking a remote and very rugged experience and called the West Coast Trail.*

Mile 160W: *Bamfield, one of the very few settlements along this coast. The Bamfield Cable Station was where the undersea telegraph cable to Australia entered the ocean.*

Mile 170W - 185W - *Barkley Sound, part of the Pacific Rim National Park, has become popular with kayakers and others seeking a wilderness travel experience. Some ships here offer to deliver kayakers to remote islands to camp, and pick them up later.*

Mile 195W - *Surf's up! Long Beach is popular with surfers in wet suits, one of the few surfing beaches accessible by road. Hardier surfers might hike with their boards through thick woods to even more remote beaches!*

Top: A painting by John Horton depicts Capt. Vancouver about to enter the Strait.

Mile 195E

This was a singular day for British Captain George Vancouver and his two ships and crews. They had sailed from England to seek the Northwest Passage from the Pacific to the Atlantic.

The sail was Captain Robert Gray, a Boston fur trader, who told Vancouver the Strait lay just inshore. Soon after, Vancouver found it: a channel 10 miles wide and 500 feet deep, leading east between high, snowy mountains. He thought it was the Northwest Passage. It wasn't, but it was another three seasons of exploring before he realized it did not exist.

At that time, Philadelphia and Boston had cobblestone streets and daily newspapers, yet the known world ended west of the Missouri River. It would be another 12 years before Lewis and Clark would set out on their journey that would reveal the dimension of the American West.

A week after entering the unknown strait, the Vancouver party, continually charting and exploring, following the shore to make sure they missed no channel that might lead to the Atlantic, turned south and entered an unknown waterway Vancouver named for one of his lieutenants, Peter Puget. Vancouver was stunned by the beauty of what he saw: hills and lowlands reaching south to the perfect volcanic cone of what he named Mt. Rainier.

When he arrived in Puget Sound and saw the myriad channels and passages leading off in all directions, it was obvious to Vancouver that the task of exploring was too difficult for his cumbersome ships, the *Discovery* and *Chatham*. The solution lay in using his 20-foot cutters, rigged to row and sail. The big boats would anchor while the small boats would set out, sometimes with Vancouver and sometimes without, charting the vast land they had discovered, one day, a few miles at a time.

For three long summers, he explored: naming and charting much of the Northwest Coast, sailing back to Hawaii each winter. He lost just one man to shellfish poisoning. It was a stunning achievement. He was just 38 years old.

NORTHWEST TIDES

As the moon pases above the maze of islands and passages that is the Northwest coast, its gravity pulls the ocean to follow it, creating the large tides here. The rise and fall of the water makes for sometimes violent currents and whirlpools in the narrow channels between the islands. The prudent mariner transits at slack water—near the time of high and low tide.

For example, several **cubic miles** of water must pass through the Discovery Islands north of Vancouver, and the San Juan and Gulf Islands to the south every six hours as the tide moves in and out. Mariners have learned to use these currents to their advantage. For instance, northbound vessels will leave Seattle at high tide, letting the north flowing ebb, with currents up to 6 mph, speed them on their way. Arriving at **Point Wilson, Mile 40** at low tide, then the north flowing flood coming in from the ocean will give them a push as they travel up into lower British Columbia waters.

Once, when I was an incautious young skipper in a 60-footer, I was towing a disabled 36-foot fishing boat from Alaska to Seattle. Eager to get home, but having missed slack water, I thought I could get through constricted **Dodd Narrows,** west of **Mile 115,** against the current. So I went up onto the flying bridge and shouldered our way into the stream.

Instantly I knew it was a mistake! The current shoved us violently back and forth and I was desperately afraid that the boat I was towing would hit the shore in one of our wild swings. Finally we got through, and I radioed back to the fellow I was towing, a cool customer, in his 25th season as an Alaska commercial fisherman.

"It wasn't too bad," he answered me, "I had to steer a bit to keep off the rocks. And I bit my cigar in half..."

Top: channel marker near Petersburg in SE Alaska. On a big high tide, the water level would rise to the top of the marker. Six hours later, it would be 20 feet lower. This creates very swift currents, making for some very challenging maneuvering around the cannery docks.

Above: this kayaker is surfing on a standing wave in a tide rip at Skookumchuck Rapids, B.C., east of **Mile 152***, where the currents rush to almost 20 mph. For a dramatic video of a tugboat capsizing when the current pushes its barge ahead of it, check out: www.youtube. com/watch?v=QEfUblSDzww*

The many logging camps and canneries that supported the old minesweeper turned freighter *Uchuck III* are pretty much gone now, replaced by floating fish farms. So the entrepreneurial owners converted the old ship yet once again to carry passengers as well as freight along these rugged and remote waterways.

Day trips out of Gold River, B.C. allow passengers a glimpse of life along these winding inlets as well as some great wildlife watching: whales and sea otters are abundant here.

Mile 195W - *Tofino: when logging was curtailed and fish runs diminished, folks thought this town might shrivel up and die. Instead it reinvented itself, thanks to surfers, kayakers, whale watchers, fish farmers, and wealthy Vancouverites seeking second homes.*

Mile 205W - *Remote Hot Springs Cove, is perfect for sweaty kakakers and fishermen!*

Mile 220W: *Nootka was a native village, home to the Nuu-chah-nulth people, where Britain and Spain agreed to a peaceable settlement to their conflicting territorial claims on the Northwest Coast.*

Mile 270W - *Kyuquot, a remote First Nations village*

Top: whale watching, ever popular on board. The boat's schedule allows it the flexibility to chase whales and cruise the shore, hoping for a glimpse of a bear as well.

Above: sea otter raft. Once they were almost totally exterminated by the Russians when they owned Alaska, killing them for their furs that were highly desired in China. Protected now, in recent years the population has rebounded mightily, much to the annoyance of commercial fishermen, as they are a major predator of valuable dungeness crabs.

Left: one of many fish farms scattered across these wilderness waterways. With floating bunkhouses for the staff and generators for electricity, they are dependent on the Uchuck III for regular delivery of fuel and supplies.

TAHSIS, MILE 260W: WHEN YOUR MILL LEAVES TOWN

Colorful entrepreneur Gordon Gibson realized something about the settlement at the mouth of the Tahsis River that only a Vancouver Island logger would know: it faced southeast, meaning that it got enough sunlight so that stored logs wouldn't start to mold before they could be exported or sawed. Plus it had deep enough water for a dock to load ships, so that logs didn't have to be first towed to Vancouver, losing many in the process.

It was a great place for a sawmill, but first he had to cut and sell enough logs to finance it. So he began logging and in just a year he had enough money to build the sawmill, milling the first boards in 1943.

The mill built, he put his carpenters to building houses for the workers, one every four days: heavy tarpaper floor, shingled roof, outhouse in the back: good enough!

Next was a school, and when the first ship, the *Tipperary Park*, arrived for the first load of lumber in 1944, the captain was amazed at the town freshly carved out of the wilderness, complete with school and store.

Just three years later the mill burned to the ground (a not uncommon fate for lumber mills and canneries), but the ashes had hardly cooled before Gibson was constructing the next one! The inlet was already almost full of log rafts waiting to be pulled out of the water and sliced into lumber. The wooded slopes of the west coast of Vancouver Island were perfect for growing big trees and the market liked his lumber. So began some very good years with ship after ship coming in to the wharf. The old logging road to the nearest town, Gold River, was upgraded and paved: folks could get out. Life was good in Tahsis!

Then came 2001: with the Japanese market for lumber suddenly in decline and new rules restricting local logging, the owner suddenly pulled up stakes, brought in a bunch of barges, loaded up all the mill equipment, and disappeared down the inlet!

The town went into shock: the population plummeted from 2500 to less than 400. Like the rest of the settlements along this remote coast, the new economic model that evolved was based on tourism and sport fishing. But the good year-round jobs were gone.

Top: when it closed down, about all that was left of the big sawmill at Tahsis was the ramp they loaded the mill equipment onto the barges with..

Middle: loading crew, 1991: these men were proud of their reputation as crews who could put on loads that wouldn't shift or get washed overboard crossing the stormy North Pacific.

Bottom: Tahsis Lumber Co. in better times.

Friendly Cove or Yuquot ("Where the winds blow from all directions) at **Mile 245W** is the home of the Mowachaht / Muchalaht people. Before the arrival of the white men starting with the Spaniards in 1774, it was the center for all the 13 tribes of this part of Vancouver Island who would gather here during the summer harvest season.

Today the tribe, still recovering from the population collapse caused by diseases brought by the first white settlers, hosts the annual Summerfest gathering where the Mowachaht/Muchalaht people have a public day of celebration following a week long campout and gathering of the tribes.

Mile 290W - *Brooks Peninsula sticks way out into the wind and the seas. Many a mariner has had a difficult time here.*

Mile 350W - *Triangle Island. An ill fated lighthouse was constructed with great difficulty here on top of a 300' cliff in 1910. The site proved way too windy; buildings had to be cabled down to avoid blowing off the cliff! Abandoned shortly thereafter, today it is a major protected bird nesting area, for example hosting probably 500,000 Cassin's Auklets, half the world's total population*

Top: detail of part of 15' tall totem.
Far left: grave of a 15 year-old.
Left: totem and pews in the church, where two cultures blend.

P. 19

"THERE WAS NOT A SOUL HERE TODAY. THE LARGE TOTEM THAT I TOOK A PHOTO OF A YEAR OR TWO AGO IS NOW LYING ON THE GROUND AND THE HOH HOH TOTEM THAT I PHOTOGRAPHED LAST YEAR HAS NOW ONE WING. SO IT GOES UNTIL AT LAST THEY ROT."

- BETH HILL, UPCOAST SUMMERS

Who was it who first brought smallpox, syphilis, and gonorrhea ashore to the natives? Was it Captain Cook's sail-maker, Captain Vancouver's gunner, an American whaler, a Spanish trader? It mattered little. A plague worse than that which swept Europe in the Middle Ages raced up and down the coast in the decades after the whites arrived.

But before that first contact, natives along this coast enjoyed the fruits of a prosperous and successful culture. And the key was simply this: the sea and the forest provided. The early white settlers had a saying for the bounty of the sea: when the tide was out, the table was set.

First of all, as compared to the interior of Canada and Alaska, the climate was mild. Mighty cedar trees provided wood for housing, for canoes, bark for clothing and baskets. The sea was full of crab, halibut, herring, candle fish (they could actually be dried and burned) but especially the salmon, which could be caught in great numbers and dried and smoked for the winter.

Typical villages were large wooden multi-family lodges, set on a protected cove. The natives traveled and traded up and down the coast in their long carved canoes, fought at times, but in general, lived in harmony with the land and, by the standard of the times, enjoyed a rich and prosperous culture.

Their wealth allowed them to create stunning works of art, in particular masks, generally used in ceremonial dances, and totem poles, used to record history in cultures without a written language.

But when the first sails of the European explorers appeared off the Northwest Coast starting in the 1750s, a curtain was about to be drawn on a powerful native culture that had endured for centuries.

By the 1890s or so, native culture was essentially collapsing, as whole villages first decimated by disease and then abandoned, just disappeared into the forests.

A Culture Lost

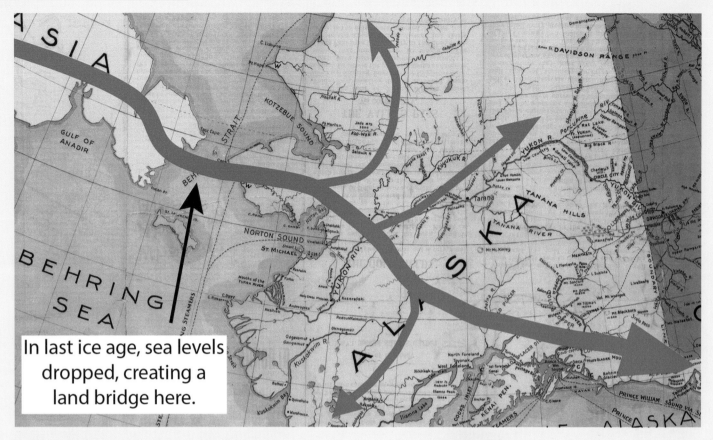

In last ice age, sea levels dropped, creating a land bridge here.

During the last ice age, thirty or forty thousand years ago, vast amounts of water was frozen in the giant glacial ice sheet that covered much of North America. This had the effect of lowering the level of the oceans so much that a land bridge between Siberia and Alaska was created across much of the shallower parts of the northern Bering Sea, and southern Arctic Ocean and Chukchi Sea.

And across this bridge, probably following the migrations of caribou and other game, came hunting parties of Siberian natives. Crossing into the New World that was North America, they eventually separated into streams that became major ethnic groupings.

These were journeys that took many thousands of years. The migration split into first two and then many streams of new settlers. The biggest division was between the bands that streamed east into the great interior of Alaska and those that traveled south and west along the coasts of Alaska, British Columbia, and US west. The interior stream moved first east and then eventually south as well to become the many tribes and bands that settled what is now the interior of the United States and Canada.

The coast streams just followed the coast wherever it led, using what was to become their traditional skin boats or umiaks - of walrus, sea lion, and seal hides, stretched over a frame of whalebone or driftwood - to cross bays and straits to colonize the islands as well. Moving further south and discovering big trees - they made their boats out of cedar, and continued their migrations and explorations.

Dancing, especially with masks, hats or other regalia, also became an important part of native culture. The dances in which the participants often wore costumes with symbolic meaning, were another way to express history or cultural events in a tribe that had no written history.

Top: Hope Island, B.C., around 1910: a typical First Nations village; a sheltered cove with canoes drawn up on the shore.

Left: Hoonah Dancers at Icy Strait Point.

Opposite: Tanu, B.C. AMNH 44310

P. 21: King-of-the-World Mask, AMNH

"We lifted the long bar from the great door of a community house, and stood, hesitating to enter. In the old days a chief would have greeted us when we stepped inside–a sea otter robe over his shoulder, his head sprinkled with white bird down, the peace sign. He would have led us across the upper platform between the house posts, down the steps into the center well of the house. Then he would have sung us a little song to let us know we were welcome, while the women around the open fires beat out the rhythms with their sticks. The earth floor would have been covered with clean sand in our honor, and cedar bark mats hastily spread for our sitting. Slaves would have brought us food - perhaps roe nicely rotted and soaked with fish oil.

"Sunlight and darkness, heat and cold, in and out we wandered. All the houses were the same size, only the house posts distinguished them. Some were without wallboards, some were without roof boards - all were slowly rotting, the remains of a stone age, slowly dying."

- *M. Wylie Blanchet, The Curve of Time.*

Top: B.C. Archives photo

GEORGE HUNT AND THE COLLECTORS

When the collectors came from the great museums of New York and Europe, they found a truly remarkable man to help them: George Hunt. His father was the manager of the Hudson Bay Trading Post in a big native village; he grew up surrounded by Kwakiutl culture, married the daughter of an influential chief, had an intimate knowledge of native traditions, and was a trusted member of the Kwakiutl community. He was able to lead the collectors deep into the wilderness to the most remote villages, to collect the stunning pieces of art that are all that remain from that era. Much fine art simply disappeared into the forest as village after village was abandoned, destroyed by the twin scourges of disease and alcoholism.

Fortunately by the late 20th century, the fortunes of many of the once impoverished and dying tribes have improved, some of the great art that was saved is being repatriated to small museums operated by the tribes, particularly in British Columbia.

Top: George Hunt and wife. AMNH 32734
Right: Undersea God. AMNH 16/771

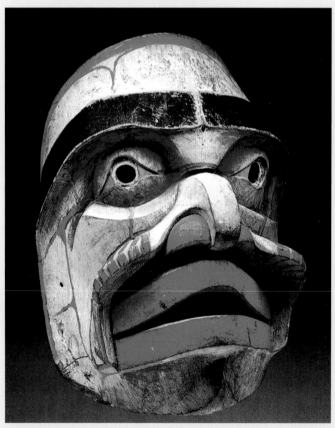

NATIVE CULTURE TODAY

By the second half of the 20th century, the fortunes of many of the coastal tribes had stabilized and begun to improve. Social programs administered by US and Canadian governments, rising prices for timber and fish - much of native income derives from fishing and logging on native land - all contributed to better living conditions.

For the tribes in Alaska, a huge event was the settlement of the Alaska Native land claims, triggered by the discovery of oil on the shores of the Arctic Ocean in far northern Alaska. In exchange for relinquishing native claims to vast tracts of land all over the state, the various tribes received substantial deeded plats of land around their ancestral homes, and a substantial cash payment.

These Alaska tribes formed corporations to manage these substantial funds, and today tribal members' income comes from a combination of fishing and woods work, and dividends from the tribal investments. In the Juneau area, for example, the Goldbelt Corporation, representing many of the natives of Southeast Alaska, built and operates the very popular tramway that runs from downtown Juneau to the top of Mt. Roberts.

Tribes in Northwest Alaska face a particular problem: the effects of global warming. In a sort of double whammy, their villages are suffering from melting permafrost - buildings sinking - and much worse: sea erosion from the loss of winter ice which traditionally protected exposed island villages. It's particularly ironic that these villagers, whose modest lifestyles do little to cause global warming, should suffer so much from it.

Top and opposite page: marchers in traditional garb at the Native Festival, a celebration of Alaska tribes, held every two years in Juneau.

Above: guide at the Mt. Roberts Tramway, owned and operated by an Alaska Native Corporation.

Vancouver

Like most Northwest coast cities, forest products played a huge part in Vancouver's history, with big square riggers waiting to take lumber to Asian, Australian, and Pacific ports as soon as it could be milled. It still continues today – you'll cross the Fraser River entering the city by bus or car. Look down and most likely you'll see B.C.'s premier product, logs, (some say marijuana is the biggest export...) traveling by barge or raft to a sawmill or a waiting ship.

With one of the best harbors on the coast, good road and rail connections, Vancouver quickly developed into Canada's premier west coast port as well. With a dramatic mountain and waterfront setting, the city became one of the favorite spots in the British Empire within a few decades of being founded, as evidenced by the many large and elegant Victorian era homes.

In more modern times, concerns about what would happen in Hong Kong after the mainland Chinese took over in 1997 led to the arrival of large numbers of Chinese immigrants, many of whom brought substantial personal wealth with them. The result is a noticeably multi-ethnic city with the second biggest Chinatown in North America.

If you have time, have a walk around Stanley Park, close to Canada Place cruise terminal, or taxi and aqua bus to Granville Island with its waterfront shopping, eating, and just enjoying the unique scene.

Opposite page top: Early morning cruise ship approaches Canada Place.
Opposite middle left: Freighter and First Narrows Bridge
Opposite right: Shopping on Granville Island
Above: Tug and log raft, Vancouver, circa 1880. John Horton painting.
Left: Totems, Stanley Park, near Canada Place.

P. 29

Georgia Strait, through which you will be traveling for almost a hundred miles leaving or approaching Vancouver, is sort of the Route One of the Inside Passage: you'll see fish boats, cruise ships, yachts, all headed to Alaska or up the British Columbia Coast.

And logs. The forest products industry of British Columbia is centered here. Immense quantities of logs travel these waters. The logs were cut deep in the forests surrounding the winding inlets, trucked to the shore, banded into bundles, and dumped into the water. Assembled into rafts of many bundles called booms, held together by cables and a perimeter of long logs or 'boom sticks' chained together, they would be towed down the long inlets and eventually to one of the mills.

For the tug crews, this was life in the slow lane: 2 or 3 mph. The hardest part was getting through the many narrow spots in the channels where the tide ran rapidly - this meant timing their trip to arrive just at slack water - the top or bottom of the tide when the current stops, only briefly.

Today however, much of the logs move up and down the coast on big barges, which travel faster and lose far fewer logs.

Look sharp at log barges and you may even see one carrying a tiny push boat to move logs around

Top: two tugs, each with a big log raft or boom, slowly working down a channel.
Right: before chain saws, loggers stood on boards (springboards) jammed into the tree! uw

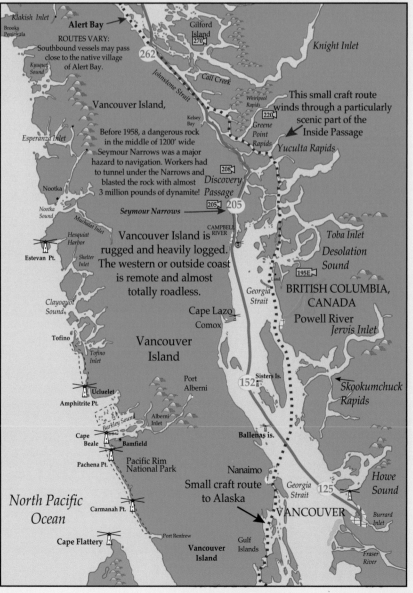

Klakish Inlet
Brooks Peninsula
Alert Bay
Gilford Island 270
Knight Inlet

ROUTES VARY: Southbound vessels may pass close to the native village of Alert Bay.

262

Johnstone Strait
Call Creek

Kyuquot Sound

Vancouver Island,

Whirlpool Rapids

Kelsey Bay

220

This small craft route winds through a particularly scenic part of the Inside Passage

Esperanza Inlet

Before 1958, a dangerous rock in the middle of 1200' wide Seymour Narrows was a major hazard to navigation. Workers had to tunnel under the Narrows and blasted the rock with almost 3 million pounds of dynamite!

Greene Point Rapids

Yuculta Rapids

Nootka

208

Nootka Sound

Discovery Passage

Mudhalat Inlet
Seymour Narrows
205
205

Hesquiat Harbor

CAMPBELL RIVER

Toba Inlet

Vancouver Island is rugged and heavily logged. The western or outside coast is remote and almost totally roadless.

Desolation Sound

Estevan Pt.
Shelter Inlet

195E

Clayoquot Sound

Georgia Strait
Lund

BRITISH COLUMBIA, CANADA

Cape Lazo
Comox

Powell River
Jervis Inlet

Tofino
Tofino Inlet

Vancouver Island

Port Alberni

152

Sisters Is.

Skookumchuck Rapids

Ucluelet
Amphitrite Pt.

Alberni Inlet

Ballenas is.

Barkley Sound

Cape Beale
Bamfield

Nanaimo

Pachena Pt.

Pacific Rim National Park

Small craft route to Alaska

Georgia Strait

125

Howe Sound

North Pacific Ocean

Carmanah Pt.

VANCOUVER

Burrard Inlet

Cape Flattery

Port Renfrew

Gulf Islands

Fraser River

Vancouver Island

L eaving port, you'll pass under the Lion's Gate Bridge. Next on your right is the Point Atkinson Lighthouse with Howe Sound beyond.

This sound, winding back into the mountain interior of British Columbia is typical of the many inlets that lead off from the main Inside Passage route: long, winding, and lonely - further north you'll pass entrances to channels and bays that might see a year pass without a human visitor.

Mile 125 - *To the south east are the Canadian Gulf Islands: rural, dry (in the rain shadow of the mountains) and very popular with boaters, and dotted with summer homes.*

Mile 152 - *On the mainland to the NE is the famous Skookumchuck Rapids, where the tidal current creates standing waves that kayakers like to surf on. See photo on P. 15.*

Mile 148- *Lasquiti Island, rumored to be popular with folks who liked to grow weed and live off the grid.*

Mile 152 - *Sisters Island Lighthouse*

Mile 160 - *The lights you may see to the east are from the big limestone mine on Texada Island. Further east, Jervis Inlet winds back into the mountains to spectacular Princess Louisa Inlet, with its dramatic waterfalls.*

Mile 173 - *To the east is the Powell River pulp mill, once one of the largest in the world. Today it just makes toilet paper.*

Mile 195 - *Cape Mudge, entrance to Discovery Passage, and site of a nasty tide rip nicknamed The Graveyard.*

Mile 295 - *Seymour Narrows - dramatic restricted canyon with sharp turn.*

Few places along the coast are as mis-named as this mini-archipelago. Granted it was rainy and raw when Captain George Vancouver named it in 1792, and he had a gloomy disposition to boot, but even if the clouds lifted only for a moment, how could he not have been stunned by these vistas?

Luckily British Columbia land managers had a better appreciation of this area and made the Sound into a protected marine park.

What's unique here is that the tidal currents, coming from both the north and the south, meet in this area. Meaning that the water level goes up and down but the same water stays, just getting warmer and warmer in the long summer days, warm enough for swimming!

Filmmaker Dan and I were here with our drone for the last week of September, 2016. On the last day the weather cleared and we found Prideaux Haven, normally crowded with boats, empty. The water was glass still and Dan jumped into the kayak and I launched the drone. From above and behind, I could see the bottom under him as his paddle made patterns like a water strider. It was exquisite.

Top photos courtesy of Dan Kowalski.

EXPLORING:
DESOLATION SOUND, MILE 190E

The Gauntlet: Yuculta Rapids Area
It's almost as if Nature put a barrier across the route north,
right in the spot where civilization ends and the wilderness begins.
As if to say: "Watch out - what lies ahead is very different from
what lies behind. Be careful!"

Devil's Hole
Dangerous Whirlpool

Dent Rapids

To Alaska

Arran Rapids

To Seattle

212E

Guillard Passage

Yuculta Rapids

Top: Yuculta Rapids area. No vessel may transit the Discovery Islands area with-out having to wait for slack water at one of the numerous tidal rapids

Above: drilling barge in Seymour Narrows with tidal rapids roaring past. A whole work crew drowned when their boat capsized in the rapids, and the attempt to blast the rock by barge was abandoned. BCARS

There's a sort of invisible line south-west to northeast through the Discovery Islands, from Seymour Narrows in the west to Yuculta and Arran Rapids in the east. Every six hours several cubic miles of water forces itself through these narrow passages as the tides flood south or ebb north.

In each place where the channel narrows, the salt water travels up to 18 MPH. As it passes over the uneven bottom, it creates violent swirls and whirlpools large enough to swallow fifty or sixty footers.

Fortunately, every six hours, at high or low tide, the current briefly stops before reversing and running hard in the other direction. This is **slack water,** which, depending on the size of the tide (which varies with the position of the moon) may last from 20 to just a few minutes. The correct time for slack water, which changes daily, is available in publications known as tide books.

When these strong currents are opposed by the wind, they create dangerously steep and breaking seas or tide rips. The rip at Seymour Narrows used to be much, much worse. A ship killer rock lurked right under the surface right in the narrowest part of the channel, skewering numerous ships and creating dangerous whirlpools that swamped many small craft.

MIGHTY SEYMOUR:
BLASTING RIPPLE ROCK

For big freighters and ships, the only route north inside of Vancouver Island was through mighty Seymour Narrows, the most constricted part of the whole Inside Passage, barely 1500' wide. Where the currents run almost 20 mph, and where before 1958, a ship killer rock lurked right in the narrowest part of the channel, creating whirlpools large enough to suck down hundred footers!

Blasting the underwater rock was an immense and hugely challenging project. At first, drillers worked from a barge anchored over the rock with four 250-ton anchors! Didn't work. The current was too strong, moving the barge and breaking off the drills.

Finally, a huge tunneling project was undertaken—boring more than 3,200 feet of tunnels and vertical shafts reaching up into the interior of the rock. This was before the invention of sophisticated surveying equipment that we take for granted today. Drillers explored with small-diameter drills until they broke through to the water. Then, they'd plug the hole and use the information to create a three-dimensional map. Finally, tugs brought 2.8 million pounds of dynamite to fill the caverns and on April 7, 1958—adios, Ripple Rock!

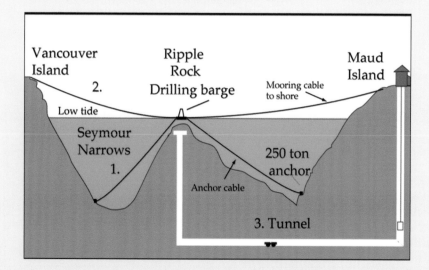

Top: Star Princess at Seymour. Ripple Rock used to be located just ahead of the ship, right in the narrowest part of the channel.
Middle: The Blast! Campbell River Museum

M. Wylie Blanchet, a single mother exploring coastal British Columbia in an old cabin cruiser, summers, in the 1930s, wrote some of the most descriptive prose about this land, in her elegiac *The Curve of Time*. It seems fitting to use some of her words to accompany these photos of a passage along part of the coast in a classic power boat:

" Yesterday, we had passed a slender Indian dugout. An Indian was standing up in the bow, holding aloft a long fishing spear poised, ready to strike. His woman was crouched in the stern, balancing the canoe with her paddle —a high, sheer cliff behind them. Cliff, dugout, primitive man; all were mirrored in the still water behind them. He struck — tossed the wriggling fish into the dugout and resumed his pose. When was it that we had watched them? Yesterday? A hundred years ago? Or just somewhere along the curve of time.

"Farther and farther into that past we slipped. Down tortuous byways—strewn with reefs, fringed with kelp. Now and then out of pity for our propeller, we poled our way through the cool, green shallows—slipping over the pointed groups of great starfish, all purple, red, and blue; turning aside the rock cod swimming with their lazy tails; making the minnows wheel and dart among the sea grapes. In other stretches herons disputed our right-of-way with raucous cries, and bald headed eagles stared silently from their dead tree perches. Once a mink shrieked and dropped his fish to flee, but instead turned to scream and defy us. "

EXPLORING: TOBA INLET

"The big house at the end of the village street had lost its roof and walls—only the skeleton remained. Its main uprights or house posts were two great wooden ravens with outstretched wings. Fourteen feet high, wing tip touching wing tip, great beaks and fierce eyes, they stared across to where, some sixty feet away, a couple of killer whales standing on their tails formed a companion pair of posts. A massive cedar log connected each pair across the tops of their heads. At right angles on top of these again, enormous cedar logs, ninety feet long and three feet in diameter, all fluted lengthwise like Greek pillars, stretched from one pair to the other, forming with the house posts, the main skeleton of the house.

"Sunlight and darkness; heat and cold; in and out (of the buildings in an abandoned Indian village) we wandered. All the houses were the same size, the same plan, only the house posts distinguished them. Some were without wall boards—all were slowly rotting, slowly disintegrating, the remains of a stone age slowly dying..."

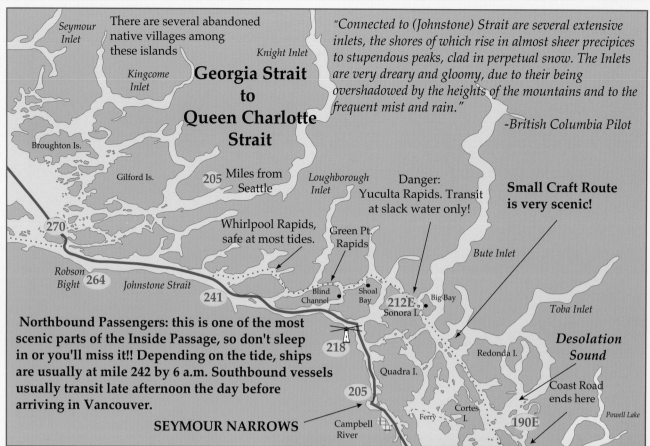

There are several abandoned native villages among these islands

Seymour Inlet

Kingcome Inlet

Knight Inlet

Georgia Strait to Queen Charlotte Strait

Broughton Is.

Loughborough Inlet

"Connected to (Johnstone) Strait are several extensive inlets, the shores of which rise in almost sheer precipices to stupendous peaks, clad in perpetual snow. The Inlets are very dreary and gloomy, due to their being overshadowed by the heights of the mountains and to the frequent mist and rain."

-British Columbia Pilot

Gilford Is.

205 Miles from Seattle

Danger: Yuculta Rapids. Transit at slack water only!

Small Craft Route is very scenic!

270

Whirlpool Rapids, safe at most tides.

Green Pt. Rapids

Bute Inlet

Robson Bight **264** Johnstone Strait

241

Blind Channel

Shoal Bay

212E
Sonora I.

Big Bay

Toba Inlet

Northbound Passengers: this is one of the most scenic parts of the Inside Passage, so don't sleep in or you'll miss it!! Depending on the tide, ships are usually at mile 242 by 6 a.m. Southbound vessels usually transit late afternoon the day before arriving in Vancouver.

218

Desolation Sound

Redonda I.

Quadra I.

Coast Road ends here

SEYMOUR NARROWS

205

Campbell River

Ferry

Cortes I.

190E

Powell Lake

Mile 185 - *Lund, the end of the coast road, cut off by the steep mountains. From here north, except for a few spots in Alaska, there are no roads along the coast; all travel is by boat or plane.*

Mile 218 - *East of here are Yuculta and Arran Rapids. Vancouver's men, exploring here, had to pull their boats through the rapids with lines from shore.*

Also along this route, popular with small craft:

Devil's Hole Whirlpool, *careless mariners have lost vessels and lives here.*

Shoal Bay, B.C. *Tiny settlement with good government dock and a pub (when they're open.) In Vietnam War days, this was the gathering point for Americans fleeing the draft and living in remote cabins.*

Blind Channel Resort - *the modest store here is one of the few places to get supplies on the Inside Passage north of Yuculta Rapids. Thoughtful loggers preserved a giant cedar in the woods nearby.*

Greene Point Rapids - *the second of a trio of tidal rapids on this route.*

Whirlpool Rapids *marks the entrance to the small craft route from the north. Most vessels will try, by taking advantage of the south flowing flood, to run all three rapids on a single tide, arriving at Yuculta, the most dangerous, at slack water.*

Right: the big cedar near Blind Slough.

Mile 264 - *Orcas come to rub their bellies on the stones of beaches here; not clear why!*

Mile 350W - *Triangle Island: the highest lighthouse on the B.C. coast built here in 1909. But it was abandoned after just a few years. Turned out it was so foggy the light was rarely seen, and so windy buildings had to be cabled down.*

Mile 375HS - *Queen Charlotte Sound: nasty place; even big Alaska ferries get beat up in winter here.*

Mile 399 - *Bella Bella native village, one of the very few settlements along this coast.*

Mile 438 - 546 - *The Northern Canyons: my nickname for this particularly narrow and winding part of the traditional Inside Passage.*

Mile 473 - *Butedale Cannery, now abandoned, but once a popular stop for tired fishermen, offering hot showers in the old bunkhouse.*

Mile 485 - *at the head of a winding inlet here is a rustic and remote hot springs. Your author stopped here with his wife to soak away the cares of long Alaska fishing seasons.*

Mile 495 - *Wright Sound: the B.C. Ferry* Queen of the North *crashed into the shore and sank here in 2006 with the loss of two passengers. The mate in charge on the bridge went to jail.*

Mile 600HS - *Dixon Entrance: another nasty place; the tidal currents pouring out of all the inlets create tide rips when the wind is blowing.*

Watch Short Videos at:

www.joeupton.com:

Mile 310 - In God's Pocket
Mile 375 - Namu
Mile 400 - Trouble in Queen Charlotte Sound
Mile 455 - The Northern Canyons
Mile 485 - Finding Bishop Bay

Want to see whales? Just keep your binoculars with you. Whales, particularly humpbacks, are seen all along the Northwest coast. And they're easy to find.

Whales are mammals, meaning they need to breathe on the surface. When they do, they exhale dramatically, creating a spout of water mixed with air that can be seen for miles, as in "Thar she blows."

Typically, whales will linger on the surface, breathing slowly, usually making shallow short dives between breaths. Then, when they lift their tail like the whale is doing in the picture to the left, it means that the whale will be "sounding," or diving deep, and may be down for as long as 15 minutes before coming up.

If you are lucky, you'll see a breach like the bottom photo in which a humpback jumps clear of the water and lands with a terrific splash that may be seen for miles.

You also may see bubble-feeding, when a group of humpbacks will circle a school of herring, breathing to create a fence of bubbles, then surface dramatically through the school, mouths open.

Orcas, or killer whales, are the other commonly seen whale. These are smaller, up to 30 feet, but are easily recognized by their tall scimitar-like dorsal fins. They are aggressive feeders, chowing down on salmon, seals, sea lions, and sometimes even smaller whales, but not humans!

Both orcas and humpbacks can be seen throughout the range that Alaska cruise ships travel.

Top: School of orcas in Johnstone Strait, B.C. Their tall dorsal fins and black and white markings make them easy to identify. Minden Pictures

Middle: A humpback lifts his tail before diving, as seen on a Juneau whale-watching tour.

*Bottom: A dramatic humpback breach in Frederick Sound, Alaska, near **Mile 845**, photographed by commercial fisherman Duncan Kowalski.*

For the mariner in small craft, traveling though the Northern Canyons, especially in the fall, is a somber, almost spiritual experience. Northbound or Southbound, you usually arrive only after getting beat up in the open waters of Dixon Entrance or Queen Charlotte Sound.

Then the mountain walls of these winding channels wrap you up. Clouds press down on the water, and you travel for two or three days. Sometimes never seeing another boat, the only sign of man the old chimney at Swanson Bay or the cannery ruins at Butedale. You pick up the anchor in the thin first light of dawn, travel until dark, anchor again close to the shore in some lonely bay, shut off the engine to hear the rush of a waterfall close in the woods. At night, stars are rare, the clouds thick, the darkness total and complete.

Top: Alaska bound troller Kestrel passing Work Island Light, **Mile 473.**
Left: your author and crew in the outside soaking tub at the Bishop Bay Hot Springs, deep in the wilderness east of **Mile 485.** *We are soaking away the cares of a long hard Alaska fishing season!*

Top: ice from Le Conte Glacier east of Petersburg, sometimes drifts into upper Frederick Sound, creating a hazard to mariners. DK photo

Above: ship in Gastineau Channel, seen from the top of the Mt. Roberts Tramway in Juneau.

The coast of Southeast Alaska, like British Columbia, is deeply indented with inlets winding far back into the mountainous and forbidding interior. The islands, large and small, form a maze of channels. In the northern part, glaciers lie at the head of many of the inlets, discharging ice year round.

Most of the area is thickly forested, without settlements or towns, little changed since the arrival of the white man. Almost all the land is owned by federal and state governments; little is available for sale to individuals.

There are a few towns. Each has a few miles of roads, few are connected to each other or to the "outside." Most travel is by boat or plane.

Scattered in little coves and harbors far from the towns are a few roadless communities that still enjoy a quiet existence. Except for storekeepers and the fish-buyers, residents mostly fish for salmon. In summer, they scatter up and down the coast, hustling to make a year's pay in a few months.

Then comes the fall. The outside boats straggle back to Washington State harbors, the days get shorter, and the sun disappears behind thick clouds. Weeks pass with only an occasional boat or float plane arriving to break the monotony.

Despite short days and gloomy weather, many local residents prefer winter. After the rush of the salmon season, winter can be a welcome change with time to work on cabin or boat, visit with neighbors, or just sit and read. It's not a fast-paced life, but there's enough to do. Many residents have spent time in the larger towns and wouldn't think of moving back.

SOUTHEAST ALASKA
Points of Interest:

1. Glacier Bay: In 1794, English explorer George Vancouver, found no bay, just solid ice all the way out to Icy Strait.

2. Lynn Canal: Surrounded by high mountains and glaciers, this waterway can be a fierce wind tunnel.

3. Admiralty Island National Monument: This area is essentially all wilderness except for the native village of Angoon. It is home to a large population of brown bears.

4. Tracy and Endicott arms: These arms lead back to glaciers, often visited by cruise ships.

5. Frederick Sound and Stephens Passage: humpbacks usually sighted here, also small icebergs are occasionally seen in this area .

6. Chatham Strait: ruins of old canneries and whale, herring, and codfish plants are still found in many of the bays here. Salmon runs remain strong but refrigerated transport vessels take the fish to towns such as Petersburg for processing.

7. Point Baker: With its population of about 35, Point Baker is one of many roadless communities scattered throughout this island archipelago. Most residents are commercial fishers. Your mapmaker built a cabin here and wrote about his many adventures in his 1976 memoir, *Alaska Blues. (And still in print!)*

8. Le Conte Bay: This is the most southerly place that a glacier reaches down to the saltwater. Off the beaten path, the rapidly retreating glacier calves its icebergs into a particularly beautiful bay.

9. Petersburg: settled by Norwegian fishermen, today this town is the commercial fishing center of SE Alaska and has a bustling waterfront lined with canneries and fish freezer plants.

10. Wrangell Narrows: a winding, 22-mile shortcut between Ketchikan and Juneau, widely used by small craft and Alaska state ferries. It is too narrow for big ships.

11. The Border Peaks: the U.S.-Canada border runs along the top of the highest peaks of the coastal range.

12. Stikine River: winds though the coastal mountains. Early gold-rush route to interior.

13. Prince of Wales Island: this is the fourth-largest island in the U.S. (after Kodiak, Hawaii, and Puerto Rico). During the heyday of logging in the 1960s, it was one of the wealthiest of Alaska zip codes. (Loggers are well paid.)

14. The Outside coast: there is only one town, Sitka, to be found on this very rough and remote 400-mile stretch of coast, seen in the map to right. Any lights you may see at night are apt to be anchored fishing boats.

15. Misty Fjords National Monument: this very rugged high country is penetrated by several deep and winding fjords. Excursions are available from Ketchikan to Rudyard Bay, a dramatic fjord.

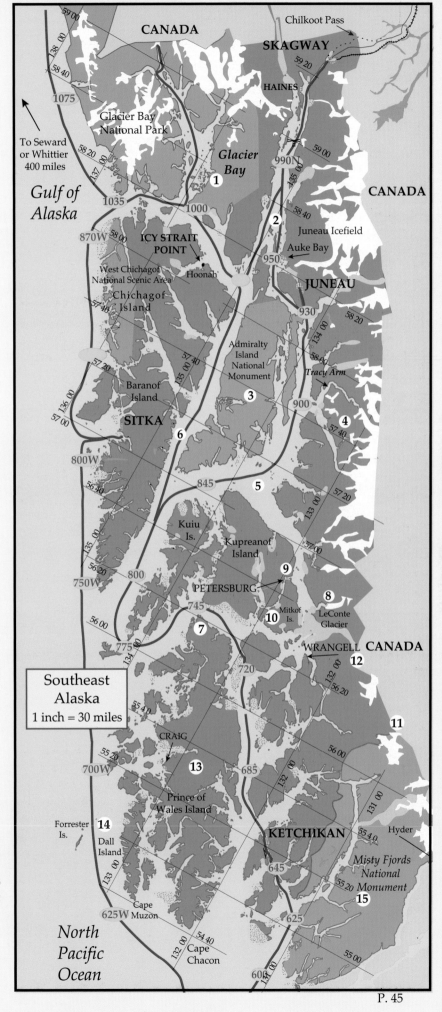

"Three Friends" Dredge on Solomon River, Alaska.

HANNAH C

ALASKA HISTORY TIME LINE

30,000 B.C.: Migratory hunters from Asia move across the land bridge from Siberia to Alaska, and settle North America.

8,000 B.C.: As the Ice Age ends, the rising ocean covers the land bridge. An ice bridge forms. Migration slows.

1741: Vitus Bering and Aleksei Chirikov land in Alaska on an expedition from Russia and take home 800 sea otter skins, but Bering is lost on the return. The fur traders begin outfitting new expeditions, and the fur rush is on.

1778: British Captain James Cook explores much of the Alaskan coast.

1792-4: British Captain George Vancouver exhaustively explores and charts the Northwest Coast with two ships.

1799: Alexander Baranov consolidates Russia's possession of Alaska with establishment of a fort and trading base at Sitka.

1867: Secretary of State William Seward buys Alaska from Russia for 2 cents an acre. Total purchase price: $7.2 million. By then, however, the valuable sea otters are almost extinct. The land deal is hailed as "Seward's Folly."

1879: Naturalist John Muir canoes throughout SE Alaska and discovers Glacier Bay. (When Captain Vancouver passed through, there was no bay to be seen, just ice.) Muir's reports inspire development of early tourism industry.

1896-1900: A gold strike on a Yukon River tributary attracts 100,000 people to the Yukon Territory and Alaska.

1922: Roy Jones makes the first float plane flight up the Inside Passage. Similar planes revolutionized bush travel in Alaska.

1925: A 674-mile dog sled relay brings diphtheria vaccine to Nome. The feat is celebrated today with the annual running of the Iditarod Trail Sled Dog Race from Anchorage to Nome.

1942: Japan invades the Aleutian Islands. The Alaska Highway project is begun to move defense supplies into the territory.

1959: Alaska becomes the 49th state.

1964: Good Friday earthquake kills 131 people in Alaska. It's a giant, the second-strongest earthquake ever recorded.

1968: Ten billion barrels of oil are discovered at Prudhoe Bay.

1971: Congress settles Alaska Native land claims, conveying 40 million acres of land and $1 billion to the state's Natives.

1976: Federal 200-mile limit established around all US coastline, sets stage for major fisheries growth in Alaska .

1977: The first oil flows through the 800-mile trans-Alaska pipeline, a monumental engineering feat.

1980: Congress passes the Alaska National Interest Lands and Conservation Act (ANILCA), establishing millions of acres of Federal park lands, wilderness areas, refuges, and other park units.

1989: The tanker *Exxon Valdez* rams a reef creating a massive oil spill and years of work for hundreds of lawyers.

2011 - US Supreme Court finally settles punitive damages to be paid by Exxon for spill, reducing award by 75%.

Opposite top; whaling ship Alexander *at the edge of the pack ice, Beaufort Sea, Alaska, circa 1895. Whalers operated off the Alaska Coast beginning in the 1850s.* UW Nowell 3.

Opposite right middle: an Aleut native gets ready to harpoon a sea otter. Otters, valued in Asia for their very thick pelt, created Alaska's first resource boom, beginning in the 1740s. The Russians treated the natives brutally, threating to destroy whole villages if the villagers didn't bring in enough pelts. UW NA1995

Opposite right lower: the next big boom was salmon, which still is a very important part of the Alaska economy. Before statehood in 1959, most salmon were caught by fish traps, owned by Seattle fishing companies. Fish traps were banned as part of Alaska's becoming the 49th state. Tongass Historical

Opposite left middle: one of many gold dredges that worked Alaska's rivers in the early to mid 1900s. UW 1796D

Opposite left bottom: visitors at an Alaska pipeline viewing area near Fairbanks. The odd looking finned structures on top are passive radiators, designed to cool the pipeline's foundations so that the permafrost below the surface doesn't melt and allow the pipeline to sink.

Right: look at these faces aboard a Yukon River paddle wheel steamer during the 1898 - 99 Klondike Gold Rush. UW Thwaites 0394-1286.

Mushers, Alaska.

EXPLORING:

Twenty miles long and two blocks wide isn't a bad way to describe Ketchikan, originally a rough–and–tumble fishing town, where Creek Street, the red-light district, was a busy place, especially on the weekends when both fishermen and loggers came into town.

The big Ketchikan Pulp Mill opened in the early 1950s, and a sawmill operated on the docks where cruise ships tie up today. It was a welcome change from the earlier days when most jobs existed only during the salmon season, and everyone lived on credit during the long winters. In pulp mill days, logging was king, and many commercial fishermen felt like second-class citizens.

Unfortunately, careless logging practices reduced salmon catches and angered commercial fishermen. Tougher logging regulations came, and the mill closed in 1997.

Fortunately, commercial fishing is strong again. The cruise industry has created many seasonal jobs. Yet, without a large-year round employer like the mill, the 8,000 or so residents of Ketchikan still find that winter can be a lean and slow time economically after the big cruise ships stop coming.

Have a look at the fishing boats in Thomas Basin, just south of downtown. Once they leave town, many boats are out for a week or more at a time. Years ago, most salmon was canned, but today a large portion gets frozen or air freighted out fresh to lower 48 markets.

A good walk is south of town - turn right off your ship - about two miles, past canneries and the Coast Guard Station, to **Saxman Village,** an authentic native community with carving shed, dancers, and numerous totems. A city bus also stops right in front; info/schedule at village office.

Opposite top: waterfront statue celebrating town history. Opposite lower right: loggers at the logging show downtown.

Lower left: Creek Street, just a short walk from downtown, is the old red light district. As they used to say, "Where the fishermen and the fish came to spawn." Don't miss artist Ray Troll's gallery - his t-shirt art is a staple of Northwest culture!

This page top: Nathan Jackson carving a new totem pole at the Saxman carving shed. Totems are made of rot resistant cedar, but still they will only last 68-80 years sitting out in the rain all the time. Left: Tlingit girl and totem, circa 1930.

Fortunately, unlike British Columbia, Alaska's fishery resources have been well managed and are generally strong. Refrigerated fish-transport vessels, or tenders, bring in fish from remote areas to processing in the towns.

Commercial fishing is tightly regulated by area, gear type, and fishing time. The return of salmon to streams is carefully monitored and fishing time tailored to make sure enough salmon return to spawn to create the next generation.

In recent years, processors have moved to build facilities to freeze more of their salmon instead of canning it, creating a higher-value product. Salmon roe, for export to Japan, has evolved to be a premium product.

Many young men and women who put themselves through college by working on Alaska fishing boats have discovered that such work makes for a great job after college as well. In the recent big years, many of the crews on good purse seiners, such as the one on the opposite page, made close to $50,000 for the three-month season while crew shares on top boats might double that!

Top: a herring skiff during the Kah Shakes Cove roe herring fishery.

Left: Your author's crew unloads at the tender, Naknek River, Bristol Bay, western Alaska. A cannery is just a half mile away, so the fish are processed quickly without needing to be refrigerated.

Top: a salmon purse seiner, which encircles schools of fish with its net, pulls the bunt, or end of the net, aboard. DK photo.

Above: valuable salmon eggs being sorted in a Petersburg cannery. The cannery boss told me jokingly that eggs were getting so valuable he was thinking of getting a guard to ride shotgun on the forklift.

Right: Many of the smaller gillnet or trolling vessels are operated by couples, or occasionally just one person.

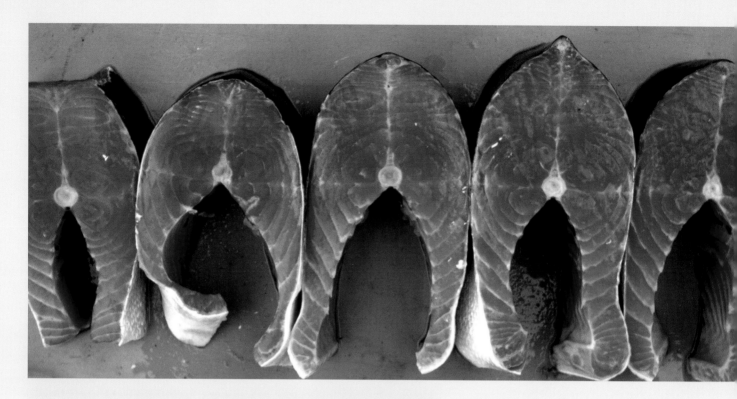

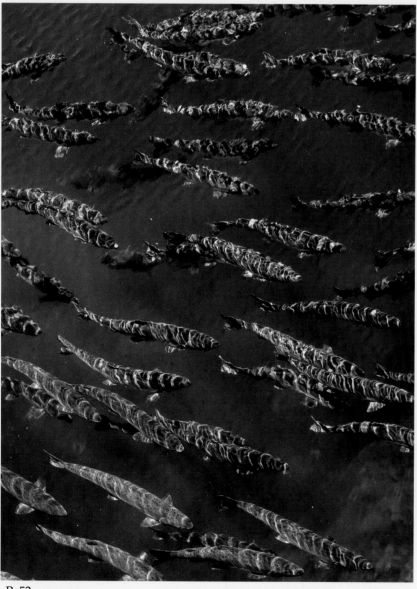

This is a salmon coast. Each year millions of small fingerlings (and older fish, depending on the species) leave Northwest streams and rivers and head out into the Pacific Ocean to make a living. Their travels might take them as far as Japan or Siberia, depending on the currents and the weather.

And then several years later, as their bodies mature and the need to reproduce arises, something truly magic happens: somehow, they return home, to the streams or lakes where they began their lives. The regular return of these fish supported first the multitude of critters that came to depend on them: bears, of course, but also seals, sea lions, minks, martens, and even raccoons.

And when the first humans came across the Bering Sea land bridge during the last ice age, they found the same species of salmon in the new world that had fed them in the old country, allowing them to more easily adapt to the new land.

Salmon first brought and supported the whites, beginning with the first canneries and salteries in the 1870s, and extending into the present where salmon is still the lifeblood of many coastal communities.

Fortunately, for the most part, in Alaska, at least, the runs remain strong. But only by fighting pollution like the proposed Preble Mine in western Alaska, can salmon's future be protected.

Top: sockeye or red salmon.
Left: pink salmon below Creek Street.

BEARS AND SALMON

When the salmon run in Alaska, first they travel up streams to their spawning grounds, then after the female lays and the male fertilizes the eggs, both fish die. Their remains comprise a major part of the yearly diet of both black and brown bears and eagles.

The largest population of bears in SE Alaska are black, up to perhaps 600 pounds. Most brown or grizzly bears live in western Alaska, though there are populations on Admiralty Island and in scattered coastal locations. "Brownies" are huge. The males weight as much as a ton!

Top and lower left: Bears at Anan Creek north of Ketchikan. Don't think you can escape a bear by climbing a tree.

Left-middle and above: Brown bears (identified by the hump on their shoulders) in the Brooks Falls area of the Katmai National Park west of Anchorage. This was a too-close encounter for our son and I!

"Ratz Harbor, Mile 695, Oct. 26, 1974 "Lured out this afternoon by a break in the weather, after two days of laying here with violent winds battering us. Big mistake - wind came up again at Narrow Pt, 2 mi. south, stirred up big tide rip; lucky to get back in here without breaking windows out. Traded booze for pork chops and instant spuds at logging camp."

Mile 685 - Meyers Chuck, pop. 21, *one of numerous roadless fishing communities, allowing very small craft to fish close to home.*

Mile 705 - Coffman Cove - pop.176, *once just a logging camp, blossomed into a community of settlers and second homes once it was connected to a road.*

Mile 710 - Honker Divide canoe trail *starts at the head of a bay to the west here. 30 rugged miles with 3 of portaging.. not for the weak hearted..*

Mile 715 - Stikine Strait *leads off to Wrangell and mouth of the Stikine River.*

Top: Breaching humpback, near **Mile 670.** *Keep your eyes peeled. Alaskastock*
Right: Sea lions near Tracy Arm. The big guy is a bull, who might weigh a ton!

Northern Clarence Straits, Mile 690 to Mile 730, is a salmon gillnet area. Boats are typically 35-45 feet long and usually operated by one or two people, often a couple. Most boats ice down their fish in their holds and deliver at the end of the Sun-Wed fishing period to fish processors in either Wrangell or Petersburg.

The gillnets used here are about 1200' long by 25' deep. Made of thin nylon dyed to match the color of the water, they are stored on a big drum in the stern. To fish, they are rolled off the drum and hang like a shallow fence in the water, catching little else except salmon.

Mile 720 - Snow Pass: Go up on the bow to look for whales! *The current in this constricted passage often concentrated herring that whales chow down on. Also look for sea lions on top of the buoy on the east side of the channel.*

Mile 730 - Wrangell Narrows *winds through the islands to the north here. Too shallow and twisting for big ships, it is much used by smaller craft, including the Alaska ferries, and saves about 90 miles between Ketchikan and Juneau.*

Top: big barge loaded with vans of canned and frozen salmon from Bristol Bay in Wrangell Narrows.

Left: fish buyer or tender loads salmon from two gillnetters near **Point Baker, Mile 745.**

Tucked into two coves south of **Mile 746** are two communities, Point Baker and Port Protection, about three miles apart, each with about 60 folks. In the 1970s, a person could lease a piece of waterfront land from The US Forest Service for a few thousand dollars a year, build a cabin with timber from the local forest, and make enough money in a boat as small as an open skiff, to get by on: pretty sweet!

These days the emphasis is more on hosting sports fishermen who stay at one of three lodges, but there still is a floating bar!

The area even has its own reality show: Port Protection.. Don't know how real it is..

Mile 745 - Mariposa Reef *is where the Mariposa, one of the finest steamers on the Alaska run ended her career in the black of a November night in 1917.*

Mile 751 - Hole in the Wall, *is one of Alaska's special places. A channel so narrow that trollers must use care if their poles are down leads to a tranquil basin where deer and bear are often seen.*

Top: Point Baker homestead.

Middle: my neighbor, Flea, around 1973. He had a little cabin on the water, his Social Security, fished every day, and grabbed a beer from the fish buyer for the run back home: not a bad retirement!

Bottom: the Point Baker floating Post Office in the 1970s. In those days the mail boat stopped around midnight on Wednesday. So on Thursday all sorts of characters would appear to pick up their mail, likely containing their weed for the week as well!

Near Point Baker we found an island, on a private cove, with a gorgeous western exposure and view, for $17,000. After the season, in our houseboat on Seattle's Lake Union, we made plans for a cabin. As our money dwindled, so did the size of our new-home-to-be until whatever roof we could get over our heads for fifteen hundred bucks would have to be it. We settled on a 12-by-16-foot box with a half loft, 275-square-feet, total: tiny.

We scoured garage sales and second-hand stores, found a big diesel oil range for $35, all our windows and doors for $175. I built a kitchen counter, complete with sink and drawers. We purchased a 16-foot cedar skiff with a 10-horsepower, 1958 Evinrude outboard. Tool by tool, fitting by fitting, we packed the supplies aboard my 32-foot gill-net vessel and skiff to tow north.

Shortly after arriving in Point Baker, the mail boat arrived with our large bundle of lumber. The plan had been to tow the tightly strapped bundle through the channel to our secluded cove and house site. But it was so green and dense, it wouldn't even float! It was what the locals called, "pond dried." So we put it temporarily on the dock and then hauled it in our skiff, load by load out the channel to our site.

We struggled to get the cabin up: the wood was so wet it splashed when your hammer missed the nail. It rained; every night we would take the skiff back to our boat at the Point Baker dock, heat up something quick, and fall, exhausted, shivering, into our sleeping bags.

And created something exquisite: out every window was the water. As we ate at the driftwood table, we could see eagles swooping, curious seals, and most marvelous of all, a pair of humpbacks that hung out in the tide rips by West Rock, off the mouth of our cove. On still nights, we could hear the sigh-like breathing of the whales as they surfaced and exchanged fresh air for stale.

We called our little cove Port Upton. We dragged huge logs off the beach, got more lumber from town to build a big float to work on our nets. Just us and our friends in that wild and remote cove.

When the first snow came one November evening, the fire in the wood stove crackled cheerily and our kerosene lamp shone out on the vast and wild world beyond the windows.

It was magic.

EXPLORING:

LONELY CHATHAM STRAIT

Mile 775 - Cape Decision Lighthouse, *is a major turning point, and the entrance to Chatham Strait. It is at the very southern tip of Kuiu Island, about the size of Maui, but with just 10 inhabitants.*

Mile 795 - Port Alexander, *is the only settlement in lower Chatham Strait. In the 1920s and 30s, with strong salmon runs, it was a money-kissed little place, where a resident once told a new arrival that it was illegal to walk the streets sober. Then the great dams on the Columbia River were built, cutting off the fish from their spawning grounds, and within a decade or so, the population of Port Alexander shrank from 2,500 to a hundred or less.*

Chatham Strait stretches for almost 150 miles, deep, wide, and today, for the most part, empty and lonely. But poke into almost any bay and you'll find evidence of a much more prosperous past. Whales, codfish, herring, and of course salmon were caught here. Whales were rendered into oil, herring into oil and fishmeal, and salmon were salted and also canned. The whaling stations, salteries, and canneries were all in remote bays, close to the resource, but distant from the nearest large town, Juneau or Petersburg. The result was that each processing plant essentially had to be a whole little town unto itself with mess halls, bunkhouses for workers, houses for management, warehouses, generators, etc.

At the head of **Big Port Walter, Mile 800**, are the buildings of the old Alaska Pacific Herring Co. now slowly falling into the bay. In the herring boom days of the 30s, 40s, and 50s, big seiners took load after load of herring here. It was also the wettest place in North America, with an average of almost 250 inches a year. What must it have been like there for the caretaker and his family, when the sun disappeared over the high mountains for months at time, and the bay froze over solid?

A few miles south is **Port Conclusion**, where Captain Vancouver and his two ships lay anchored in August, 1794, waiting for his smaller boats filling in the last blank places on his chart of Southeast Alaska. Finally on the 19th they showed up. So with grog for all hands and cheers ringing from ship to ship so far from England, there ended one of the most remarkable feats of exploration in modern times. In three long seasons of charting this unknown (to whites..) coast, through persistent fogs, strong currents, even icebergs, Vancouver had disproved the ages-old notion of a Northwest Passage through the continent back to the Atlantic.

I saw the Strait first when I was 19, working on an Alaska fish boat. I'd get the night watches, down Chatham. I'd turn down the lights on the radar and instruments until I could just make out the dim loom of the high land on either side of the strait. All that shore, all that land, but never a light or a boat; for a kid, raised on the urban East Coast, it was stunning.

LEVIATHAN OF THE DEEP
SPERM WHALE 65 FEET LONG SWC PORT ARMSTRONG ALASKA R.S. GEN

Mile 790 - Port Armstrong *was the site of a whaling station, today just ruins.*

Mile 805 - Big Port Walter *was a major herring plant in the 1940s and 50s, also the wettest place in the mainland US.*

Mile 807 - Tebenkof Bay, *was a popular spot for small salmon trollers, with its protected arms and a fish buyer also selling fuel and groceries.*

Bay of Pillars, Mile 815, *was the site of yet another cannery, now just pilings on the beach and some rusty tanks and boilers. At the head of the bay a big anchored tug, the Sea Ranger, serves as a base lodge for fly-in sports fishing groups.*

A veteran's organization, Bay of Pillars, Inc. has built a lodge on the site of the old cannery to provide wilderness experiences for veterans and their families.

Mile 828 - Washington Bay, *is narrow and steep sided, and the site of the ruins of yet another abandoned cannery*

Top: a big sperm whale hauled out on the slipway at **Port Armstrong, Mile 790,** *around 1930.* Mohai 15329

Left: troller Kestrel at the narrow entrance to **Big Port Walter, Mile 805.** *The Standard Oil tanker used to steam up this channel to deliver fuel to the herring plant up at the head of the bay.*

Opposite top: Cape Decision lighthouse

Opposite lower: an old timer at Port Alexander remembers the glory days.

P. 59

EXPLORING:
BAIRD GLACIER

In August, 2014, we stopped in here aboard the small ship, *Wilderness Adventurer*. As you can see, receding glaciers change substantially as they melt. We were fortunate; after we climbed the 60' terminal moraine - where the glacier had stopped, leaving a hill of rocks and debris that it had pushed ahead of itself - we found that the melt water pool that had blocked hikers the year before, had drained away, allowing us to actually climb up and walk around the austere moonscape that was the top of the glacier.

The US - Canada border runs through the rugged mountains of the coastal range north and east of Baird Glacier. Two notable peaks, popular with climbers are the **Devil's Thumb, 9,077'**, and **Kate's Needle, 10,002'**.

Top: your author and wife, Mary Lou, near a melt pool on the top of Baird Glacier, northeast of Petersburg. The day before, Mary Lou and a group of passengers hiked far back into the wilderness east of Thomas Bay to where kayaks had been dropped by chopper so they could paddle a lake in front of a glacier.
Right: the moonscape that is a receding glacier!

Helped by a harbor too small for the big ships, Petersburg town fathers decided to just do what they do best: catch and process fish. Settled by Norwegian immigrants, who'd fished in the old country, they felt right at home here with the dramatic mountains and strong fishery resources.

Just north of cannery row, modest houses lined the street overlooking Wrangell Narrows and Frederick Sound. From their living rooms and dining tables, the families could look out at the boats headed home from the fishing grounds. After work the men could stroll home along the water. Not a bad life.

Ole Sjonning Husvik
1890 - 1961
"Ya, vi ha it god in America"

THE FIRST ICE:

LE CONTE BAY

Top: Le Conte bergs with Horn Cliff, across Frederick Sound from Petersburg in the background.

Above: grounded berg: the tilted flat part was on the surface, the rest was all underwater until the tide went out, giving a better sense of just how much of a berg is underwater!

Off the beaten path, hidden in the coastal mountains east of Petersburg, is Le Conte Bay. It's a stunning spot—one of Alaska's secret places—but with unpredictable, rapidly changing weather, and swiftly flowing tides. The bay presented challenging conditions for filmmaker Dan Kowalski and me.

But we found a place on the beach to set up the video cameras and audio recorder. At the edge of the place where we were filming was a small beached iceberg, about the size of a dump truck. I was thinking of going over and leaning against it. But before I could, the iceberg suddenly collapsed with big chunks crashing onto the very place I would have been standing.

I was lucky that day. But that close call was a reminder that the wilderness is always waiting—for the foolish, for the careless, and or just the unlucky.

In the early evening, after the current eased, we anchored away from the ice, and climbed into the skiff to go out among the big bergs.

We let the sun get a little lower, find some clouds to diffuse it, and suddenly we had that moment with the perfect soft light that filmmakers wait for.

We turned the motor off, and I let the currents push us in a slow circle among the bergs while I talked and Dan filmed. It was perfect.

We shot until dusk, then it was time to pick our way through the bergs in the failing light and get across lower Frederick Sound to a safe anchorage. It was black before we got clear, and I was cooking with just a dimmed headlamp so as not to disturb Dan's night vision, least he T-bone one of the floating pieces of ice, which by then were essentially invisible.

In the foggy black, guided only by the eerie pale shapes on our radar screen and plotter, we found a safe anchorage in the protection of a dot of an island, dropped the anchor, and shut everything down to savor the welcome silence.

When it was coffee time the next morning, we looked out at such a lovely and peaceful sight: the few acres of island just emerging from the dawn sunlit fog, with seals popping up curiously around us, and the cry of crows and ravens in the trees.

RUNNING IN ICEBERG TERRITORY

Upton's Log

"Oct 6, 1982 - Dawn, Frederick Sound, south of **Mile 870**: We'd been passing ice - small bergs and drift ice - on and off since midnight. A sliver moon gave us just enough light to see the biggest bergs. But then it got foggy, and my heart was in my throat - my pregnant wife is aboard, and most of a berg is underwater, extremely hard to see even with the best radar.

If we were just a regular gill-netter, we'd have anchored up and waited for daylight. But we were a salmon buyer, deep in the water with 120,000 pounds and the cannery wants them quick, so on we go. We turn off the compass light, the instruments, even the running lights to allow our eyes to get accustomed to the dark, to hope to see a berg in time.

A few years earlier, a friend was running in fog with another big load of fish. He had a good radar, but it was a moonless night and the berg he hit probably wasn't much bigger than a fridge or a tub, totally invisible on radar. But it smashed in his wooden bow, and they sank with just enough time to jump into the skiff."

Top: running in ice country.
Right top: trying to get out of Le Conte at last light. (Story on previous page)
Right lower: the next morning: whew.. no ice in sight.

Small ships offer a much more intimate experience than large ones. This is the *Wilderness Adventurer*, carrying about 50 passengers on a week-long cruise between Ketchikan and Juneau.

Typically such cruises will concentrate less on the ports and anchor up to explore places where passengers may hike and kayak, usually with no one else in sight. This was 2014, a particularly warm summer with just one sunny day after another.

Every morning we'd start with yoga on the back deck, have a great breakfast, and head out for the activity of the day. It might be hiking, kayaking, snorkeling one day, even swimming for the hardy.

For information: Uncruise.com

Mile 845 - *The village visible to the southeast is* **Kake***, a Tlingit native village, pop. around 600. A small fish processing facility provides markets for the local fishermen.*

Mile 870 *is about the northern limit for icebergs that have drifted from Le Conte Glacier, 55 miles east.*

Mile 895 - Point Astley - *a major sea lion rookery. We visited here in 2012, and counted almost 100 of the big bruisers.*

Top: launching kayaks in Misty Fiords.
Right: getting a few paddling tips.

Once I was in one of the ship's kayaks, in a creek mouth with thousands of salmon waiting to spawn. One of the guides saw what was happening and radioed to the ship where a couple was just relaxing in the hot tub after a long hike. Passing them flippers, snorkels, and masks, he told them to keep their bathing suits on and jump into the inflatable with him (this was a hot summer, and the creek waters were warm enough for swimming.) He buzzed over to the creek where I was paddling and they jumped in with the fish.

Of course the salmon were startled at first, but quickly got used to the snorkelers, who were treated to the stunning experience of being eye to eye with thousands of salmon!

Top: kayaking near Dawes Glacier, at the head of Endicott Arm. The telephoto lens makes the face of the ice seem close. Don't worry; we gave it a good berth, as we knew that bergs can drop into the water without warning, creating dangerous waves!

Left: hikers coming ashore at Thomas Bay to hike three miles and kayak in the lake below yet another glacier.

Exploring:

Fords Terror

Little visited **Fords Terror** (named for a Navy crewman who, paddling into the inlet, was terrified by the violent tidal currents) is a dramatic fjord near regularly visited **Tracy Arm, Mile 900**. The tidal rapids in the entrance are dangerous to small craft and should only be attempted at slack water. I traveled there for the first time in my 32' salmon gill-netter:

Sept 5, 1972 - Just at 1, and with little water under us and at dead slow, we transited the rapids in the creek-like entrance to Fords Terror. Hardly spoke a word for the next mile, so dramatic was the scenery. The channel was scarcely a hundred feet wide. To the north a sheer rock wall rose a thousand feet before sloping back out of sight. To the south was a rocky beach rising rapidly to dark forests and snowy peaks. Old John Muir was the first white man here in the 1870s. He was so awed by the scenery he named it Yosemite Inlet, and don't think there have been too many visitors since. We passed a waterfall that was falling at least a hundred feet into the trees below. The gorge opened up to a basin perhaps a half mile by a half mile, and we dropped the hook and walked until our boat was just a dot on the far shore.

The sun went over the mountain at 4:30 and the evening came early and chill. At dusk, flight after flight of ducks came in low and fast, to settle on the water near the shore with the rush of many wings and soft callings.

Night came chilly, with northern lights again. Stood on the deck and watched the birds with Susanna until the cold drove us in. Yesterday and today, the places we visit make us feel small indeed."

"Sept 6 - First frost! The stove went out in the night and we woke to find the dog nestled in between us. To go out on the frosty deck on such a morning with the still, glassy basin around us, and dark forests and frozen hills above—words can't tell it, pictures can't show it."

THE BAD ICEBERG

In June of 2011, filmmaker Dan Kowalski and I found this stunning iceberg at the mouth to Fords Terror, about 200' long with an arch 30' high. Now, Dan and I are very experienced; we know how suddenly and easily bergs can capsize. But we assumed this one, from where it was laying, was grounded, (sitting on the bottom) and therefore stable.

Jumping in the small outboard inflatable skiff with our cameras, we circled that gorgeous iceberg in awe, stopped the engine and drifted, close to the arch, but being savvy guys, not underneath. It was a Zen-like experience: we could feel the berg's cold breath on our faces, hear the hiss of bubbles rising from the submerged mass below us. The blue translucent arch just towered over us, seemingly lit from within. The sea was still; in the distance was the whisper of the waterfall tumbling down the canyon wall: a magic moment.

Then there was this rumble that we felt more through the water than heard. Dan turned to me with a smile, "The iceberg is talking to us."

A moment later the iceberg broke in half, just at the top of the arch, almost directly over our heads. Stunned into inaction, our cameras hanging from our necks, we gasped as the nearer half rolled toward us, all in slow motion, smacking into the water just behind our outboard. Only when the other half rolled away and the previously underwater part emerged from the water under us, shoving water into our boat and pushing us back, did we have the presence of mind to start the motor and dart away, lest an ice projection catch our boat and flip it.

"Well," Dan said, when we'd gotten away from the now two bergs and caught our breath, "what was the worst that could have happened? We'd have been in the water, our cameras would have been toast, but we could have flipped the boat back over, and paddled the half mile back to where the *Sue Anne* was anchored and warmed up there..."

Or not, I thought...

So take it from a couple of really experienced guys: don't get close to icebergs in small craft!

Exploring:

Tracy Arm

Tracy Arm, a winding fjord close to Juneau, is both an alternate stop for ships unable to get a permit to visit Glacier Bay and a destination for Juneau-based excursions.

Many ships enter Tracy Arm early in order to make a port stop in Juneau later the same day. **Tip:** If your ship has a schedule like this, be sure to get up in time to see the entrance, and in particular the dramatic right-angle turn.

Also, look for glacial striations along the sides of the fjord. These are long scars or gouges, parallel to the water that were created when rocks embedded in the glacier were carried with it as it moved down from the snow fields in the mountains, grinding grooves into the fjord walls.

Occasionally, because of fog or too much ice in Tracy Arm, ships will visit Endicott Arm to the south instead and get as close to the ice at Dawes Glacier as they can.

Top: What's wrong with this photo? (Except for no life jackets; we were way too casual back then...) Actually, getting this close to a big iceberg is very risky, as they can roll over without warning, creating waves small enough to capsize small craft like this..

Right: passengers from a small ship explore the steep shore of Tracy Arm.

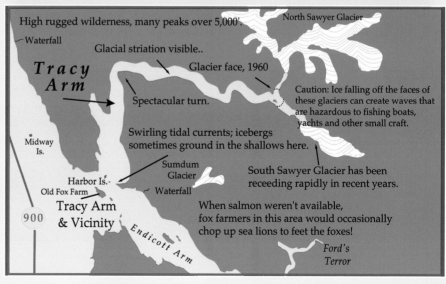

High rugged wilderness, many peaks over 5,000'.

North Sawyer Glacier

Waterfall

Glacial striation visible..

Tracy Arm

Glacier face, 1960

Spectacular turn.

Caution: Ice falling off the faces of these glaciers can create waves that are hazardous to fishing boats, yachts and other small craft.

Midway Is.

Swirling tidal currents; icebergs sometimes ground in the shallows here.

Sumdum Glacier

South Sawyer Glacier has been receding rapidly in recent years.

Harbor Is.
Old Fox Farm

Waterfall

Tracy Arm & Vicinity

When salmon weren't available, fox farmers in this area would occasionally chop up sea lions to feet the foxes!

900

Endicott Arm

Ford's Terror

Top: aboard the small ship Spirit of Oceanus, *you can see how steep the sides of the fjord are.*

Above: Entering Tracy Arm.

Right: don't try this at home.. Dogs don't like to be dropped off on little icebergs. He kept barking and barking until we returned and picked him up.

Downtown Juneau
and vecinity

Last Chance Basin and
Mining Museum

Flume Walking Trail

Governor's
Mansion

Cruise Ship Docks

JUNEAU

A bear? Behind the espresso stand? No roads in or out? You can only get there by boat or plane? What kind of a state capital is this?

Almost surrounded by high mountains and with a vast ice field—larger than Rhode Island—to the north, Juneau winters are substantially colder than those of Ketchikan or Sitka. Tlingit natives had fish camps near where downtown is today, but wintered in a more temperate and sheltered area near Auke Bay.

Alaska's first gold rush started here in 1880, but after the easy-to-find stream bed gold was gathered quickly, industrial-scale, deep tunnel mining was needed to follow the veins far underground. Massive stamp mills were built to extract gold; it wasn't uncommon for 20 or more tons of ore to be dug and processed to yield a single ounce of fine gold. The tailings—the crushed rock that was left—were dumped along the shore, creating the flat land on which today's downtown Juneau was built.

At peak capacity, the big stamp mills of the Alaska-Juneau mine, still visible above the cruise-ship docks, could crush 12,000 tons of ore a day. Working conditions were dangerous. The entrance to the big Treadwell mine was nicknamed the "Glory Hole," for all the miners—sometimes one a week—that went to glory there. Eventually the gold played out, the tunnels—by then down to 2,100 feet below the channel—filled with water, and today all that's left are ruins and miles of tunnels.

If you see Build The Road bumper stickers around town, they're about a plan to build a road up the east side of Lynn Canal to connect to a ferry dock, where you could take a short ferry to Skagway, where there is a road out to the rest of the world. However, the geography is so steep and winter weather so challenging that it might not happen for a long, long while.

Right: native woman and ceremonial mask at a Juneau gallery.

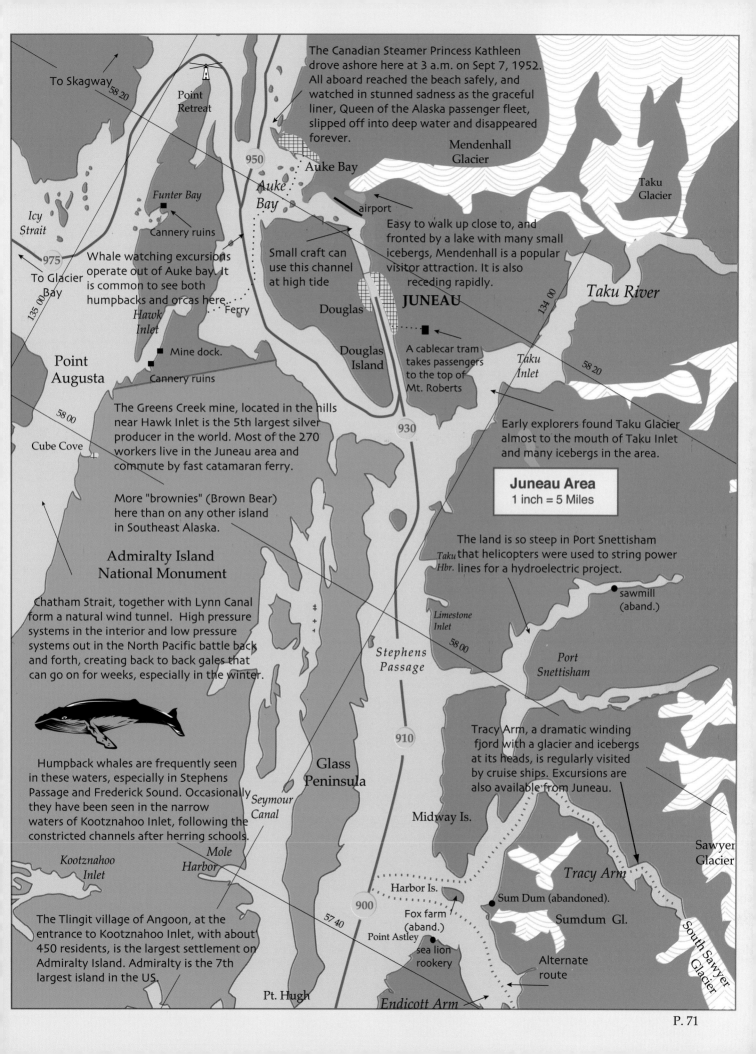

To Skagway *58 20*

Point Retreat

The Canadian Steamer Princess Kathleen drove ashore here at 3 a.m. on Sept 7, 1952. All aboard reached the beach safely, and watched in stunned sadness as the graceful liner, Queen of the Alaska passenger fleet, slipped off into deep water and disappeared forever.

Mendenhall Glacier

Taku Glacier

950

Auke Bay

Auke Bay

airport

Funter Bay

Icy Strait

Cannery ruins

975

Whale watching excursions operate out of Auke bay. It is common to see both humpbacks and orcas here.

Easy to walk up close to, and fronted by a lake with many small icebergs, Mendenhall is a popular visitor attraction. It is also receding rapidly.

Taku River

135 00

Hawk Inlet

Ferry

Douglas

JUNEAU

134 00

Taku Inlet

58 20

Small craft can use this channel at high tide

Point Augusta

Mine dock.

Douglas Island

A cablecar tram takes passengers to the top of Mt. Roberts

Taku Hbr.

Cannery ruins

58 00

The Greens Creek mine, located in the hills near Hawk Inlet is the 5th largest silver producer in the world. Most of the 270 workers live in the Juneau area and commute by fast catamaran ferry.

Early explorers found Taku Glacier almost to the mouth of Taku Inlet and many icebergs in the area.

Cube Cove

Juneau Area
1 inch = 5 Miles

More "brownies" (Brown Bear) here than on any other island in Southeast Alaska.

The land is so steep in Port Snettisham that helicopters were used to string power lines for a hydroelectric project.

Admiralty Island National Monument

sawmill (aband.)

Chatham Strait, together with Lynn Canal form a natural wind tunnel. High pressure systems in the interior and low pressure systems out in the North Pacific battle back and forth, creating back to back gales that can go on for weeks, especially in the winter.

Limestone Inlet

58 00

Port Snettisham

Stephens Passage

910

Tracy Arm, a dramatic winding fjord with a glacier and icebergs at its heads, is regularly visited by cruise ships. Excursions are also available from Juneau.

Humpback whales are frequently seen in these waters, especially in Stephens Passage and Frederick Sound. Occasionally they have been seen in the narrow waters of Kootznahoo Inlet, following the constricted channels after herring schools.

Glass Peninsula

Sawyer Glacier

Seymour Canal

Midway Is.

Kootznahoo Inlet

Mole Harbor

Tracy Arm

Harbor Is.

Sum Dum (abandoned).

900

The Tlingit village of Angoon, at the entrance to Kootznahoo Inlet, with about 450 residents, is the largest settlement on Admiralty Island. Admiralty is the 7th largest island in the US.

57 40

Fox farm (aband.)

Point Astley

sea lion rookery

Sumdum Gl.

Alternate route

South Sawyer Glacier

Pt. Hugh

Endicott Arm

THE HILLS ARE HONEYCOMBED WITH TUNNELS!

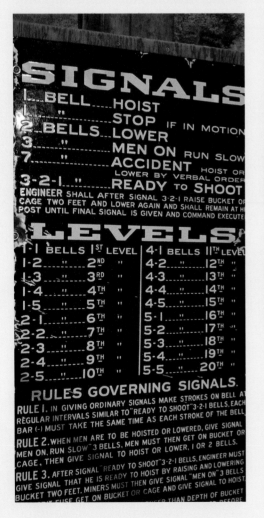

SIGNALS

	BELL	HOIST	
	"	STOP	IF IN MOTION
2	BELLS	LOWER	
3	"	MEN ON	RUN SLOW
7	"	ACCIDENT	HOIST OR LOWER BY VERBAL ORDER
3-2-1	"	READY to SHOOT	

ENGINEER SHALL AFTER SIGNAL 3-2-1 RAISE BUCKET OF CAGE TWO FEET AND LOWER AGAIN AND SHALL REMAIN AT H POST UNTIL FINAL SIGNAL IS GIVEN AND COMMAND EXECUTE

LEVELS

1-1	BELLS	1ST	LEVEL	4-1	BELLS	11TH	LEVEL
1-2	"	2ND	"	4-2	"	12TH	"
1-3	"	3RD	"	4-3	"	13TH	"
1-4	"	4TH	"	4-4	"	14TH	"
1-5	"	5TH	"	4-5	"	15TH	"
2-1	"	6TH	"	5-1	"	16TH	"
2-2	"	7TH	"	5-2	"	17TH	"
2-3	"	8TH	"	5-3	"	18TH	"
2-4	"	9TH	"	5-4	"	19TH	"
2-5	"	10TH	"	5-5	"	20TH	"

RULES GOVERNING SIGNALS.

RULE I. IN GIVING ORDINARY SIGNALS MAKE STROKES ON BELL AT REGULAR INTERVALS SIMILAR TO "READY TO SHOOT" 3-2-1 BELLS, EACH BAR (-) MUST TAKE THE SAME TIME AS EACH STROKE OF THE BELL

RULE 2. WHEN MEN ARE TO BE HOISTED OR LOWERED, GIVE SIGNAL MEN ON, RUN SLOW" 3 BELLS, MEN MUST THEN GET ON BUCKET OR CAGE, THEN GIVE SIGNAL TO HOIST OR LOWER, 1 OR 2 BELLS.

RULE 3. AFTER SIGNAL "READY TO SHOOT" 3-2-1 BELLS, ENGINEER MUST GIVE SIGNAL THAT HE IS READY TO HOIST BY RAISING AND LOWERING BUCKET TWO FEET. MINERS MUST THEN GIVE SIGNAL "MEN ON" 3 BELLS FUSE GET ON BUCKET OR CAGE AND GIVE SIGNAL TO HOIST THAN DEPTH OF BUCKET

Literally hundreds of miles of tunnels were drilled in the hills behind Juneau and even the channel in front, in the search for gold. Large rooms were created as the ore was excavated, with pillars supporting the ceiling and the rooms and pillars of levels above them.

But then as the richer ore was depleted, mine operators began to **shave down the pillar**s to recover the richer ore within them. Bad move; the mining of pillars in the Treadwell Mine, underneath Gastineau Channel, led to a sinkhole opening up right at the edge of the water, as the tide was coming up! The salt water ran into the mine with such force that the escaping air blew the elevator house totally off the mine, which was never reopened. Luckily no one died. And World War I was waiting for the laid off miners.

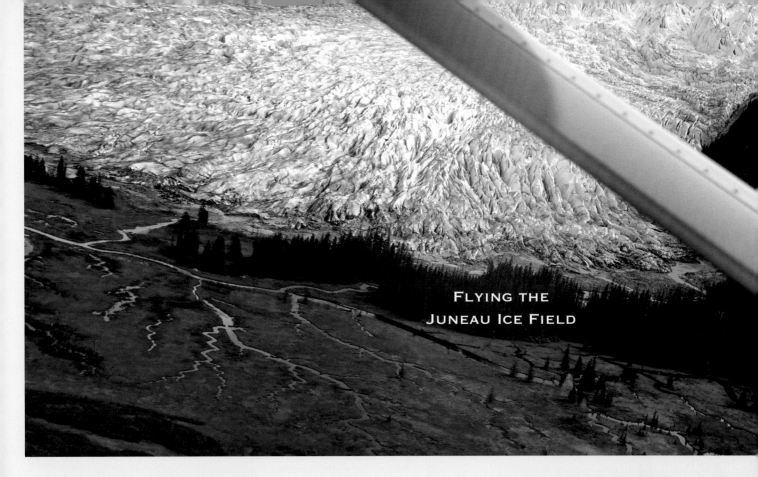

FLYING THE
JUNEAU ICE FIELD

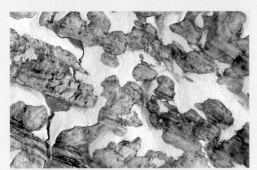

Behind Juneau is a vast ice field with fascinating shapes and colors. Flight seeing excursions are offered both by the big new turbo Otter float planes and by helicopter. The tours come in several flavors. The helicopter excursions usually land and encourage passengers to explore the top of the glacier on foot. Additionally, you may choose to take a helicopter to a dog-sledding camp set up on the glacier and experience dog sledding first hand. The dogs really get excited when the choppers land, as they know they'll soon be able to their favorite thing: pull, pull, pull!

The float planes offer both a scenic flight and one combined with a salmon dinner at a waterfront lodge.

Mile 951: Point Lena, *was the last resting place for the crack liner,* Princess Kathleen. *She ran ashore in 1957. All climbed down to shore, but the graceful liner slipped off into deep water.*

Mile 962: Sentinel Island, *was almost the end of the graceful steamer* Princess May *as well. She ran ashore in 1910, but no one was injured and she was repaired and returned to service.*

Mile 966: Vanderbilt Reef *was the site of the 1917 loss of the* Princess Sophia. *On her last run of the season, in a blinding snowstorm she drove up on the reef. Rescue boats arrived to take passengers off, but the ship seemed stable, so the* Sophia's *captain decided to wait for better weather. Bad choice: the wind drove the ship off the reef in the night, drowning all 243 souls.*

Nor are modern ships immune: Mile 972, Poundstone Rock *was the place where the huge* Star Princess *grounded in 1995, causing 27 million dollars of damage. 12 years later, the paddle-wheeler* Empress of the North *ran aground on Hanus Reef further north in the canal. Both these two last accidents happened despite both ships having modern electronic navigation equipment.*

Top: Princess May; *see text above.* UW

More than any other waterway in Southeast Alaska, Lynn Canal is a wind tunnel. The southern part of the Canal opens directly into Chatham Strait, creating this 200 mile long canyon. North Pacific lows roar up from the south and Alaska Interior highs roar down from the north. The effect is that sometimes you get a nasty gale from the south followed by an equally nasty gale from the north with hardly any time in between. But if you're on a cruise ship, no worries; summers are usually gale-free.

"**Lynn Canal, Oct. 2, 1973** - Comes with NW gale driving down off the vast cold mainland to the north. Sleet turned to snow after midnight, blotting out the lights of the boats around us. Picked up net at first light in driving snow, ice building up on the cork line. But it had almost a hundred salmon; that's a thousand bucks that looks mighty good in February. My wife stays inside when I pick the net on these really nasty nights, cozy with the dog on the bunk; don't blame her.

Picked last set up before noon in stinging snow, had to turn away from the wind and just wait for squalls to pass. The wind was blowing the tops off the seas and slopping them into the cockpit. So glad to finally get net all in, get inside, and change into dry clothes by the cozy stove. Wipers froze and started making ice on the rigging as well.

Bucked at half speed for three hours before the land came out of the snow with two fish buying boats snuggled up against the shore, their deck lights on in mid-afternoon, the hills behind disappearing in snow squalls. We are the last boat to unload, then they were gone, lost almost at once in the gloom and swirling snow, 200 long miles down to the cannery.

Ran up to the head of the cove and tied alongside three friends with all our anchors out. Night came quick with 15 boats crowded into this tiny anchorage. Weather wild out there, but cozy enough in here with salmon baking, Susanna beside me and the good doggie snoring on the floor. Violent squalls again at 9, laying us all over with their power, lines and fenders creaking."

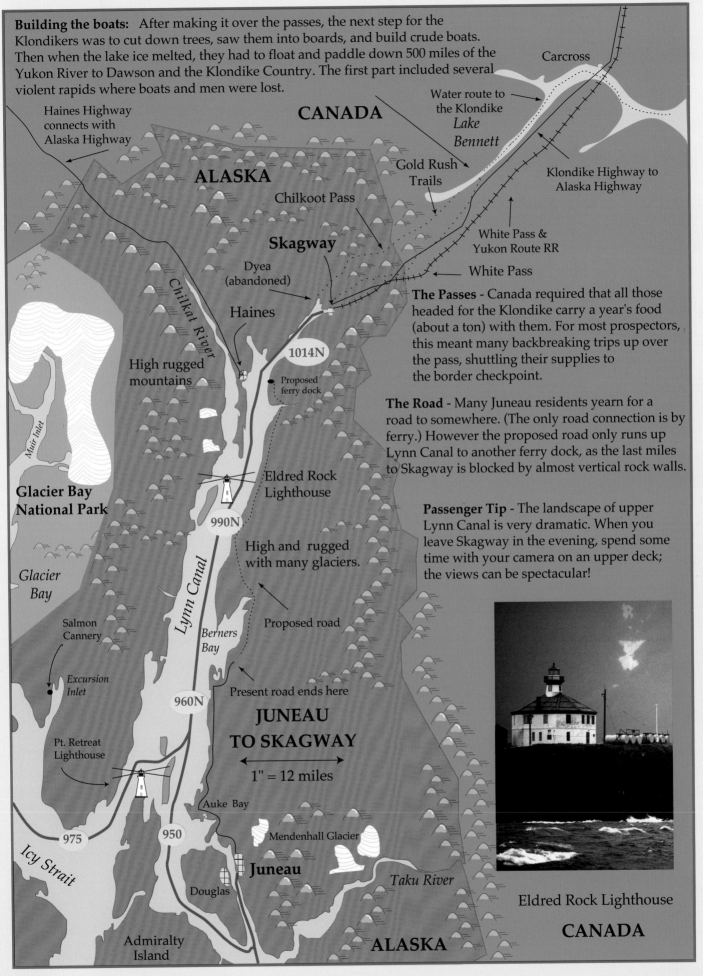

Building the boats: After making it over the passes, the next step for the Klondikers was to cut down trees, saw them into boards, and build crude boats. Then when the lake ice melted, they had to float and paddle down 500 miles of the Yukon River to Dawson and the Klondike Country. The first part included several violent rapids where boats and men were lost.

Carcross

CANADA

Water route to the Klondike
Lake Bennett

Haines Highway connects with Alaska Highway

ALASKA

Gold Rush Trails

Klondike Highway to Alaska Highway

Chilkoot Pass

Skagway

Dyea (abandoned)

White Pass & Yukon Route RR

White Pass

Haines

Chilkat River

1014N

Proposed ferry dock

The Passes - Canada required that all those headed for the Klondike carry a year's food (about a ton) with them. For most prospectors, this meant many backbreaking trips up over the pass, shuttling their supplies to the border checkpoint.

High rugged mountains

The Road - Many Juneau residents yearn for a road to somewhere. (The only road connection is by ferry.) However the proposed road only runs up Lynn Canal to another ferry dock, as the last miles to Skagway is blocked by almost vertical rock walls.

Muir Inlet

Eldred Rock Lighthouse

990N

High and rugged with many glaciers.

Glacier Bay National Park

Passenger Tip - The landscape of upper Lynn Canal is very dramatic. When you leave Skagway in the evening, spend some time with your camera on an upper deck; the views can be spectacular!

Glacier Bay

Proposed road

Salmon Cannery

Berners Bay

Lynn Canal

Excursion Inlet

960N

Present road ends here

Pt. Retreat Lighthouse

JUNEAU TO SKAGWAY

1" = 12 miles

Auke Bay

975

950

Mendenhall Glacier

Icy Strait

Juneau

Douglas

Taku River

Eldred Rock Lighthouse

Admiralty Island

ALASKA

CANADA

THE GOLD RUSH:
WHAT THEY FACED
WHO STRUCK IT RICH

For some the challenge of The North - the cold, the conditions, was simply too much:

"It was a real cold night. We walked along in the snow and we come to a fellow setting on the back of a Yukon sled. Yep, he was sitting there in the middle of the road talking to hisself. He looked plumb played out. He never seen us: he just went on talking to hisself. Over and over he'd say: 'It's hell. Yes; multiply it by ten and then multiply that by ten, and that ain't half as bad as this is. Yes, it's hell...'"

- Martha Mckeown, The Trail Led North
Drawing by Christine Cox

The headlines spread like a prairie fire across a depression ravaged country: "GOLD, GOLD, GOLD! Greenhorns struck it rich, even the inexperienced coming home with fortunes."

Farmers dropped their plows, storekeepers, mill, and factory workers with good jobs took off their aprons and walked out, men left their families.

And started traveling west. Some went through Canada, but most got to San Francisco, Portland, or Seattle, where merchants had set up shop along the waterfront to show and sell them what they needed to get to the faraway Yukon and strike it rich.

Ship owners pulled old derelicts off the mudflats, jury rigged the engines back together, loaded them up with gold hungry men and sent them north. A few ships went the very long way up the Inside Passage and then across the Gulf of Alaska to enter the Bering Sea at Unimak Pass, almost 2000 miles from Seattle. There they'd transfer to a shallow draft paddle-wheeler for another 2500 miles up the Yukon River and finally to Dawson and the Klondike River.

But most streamed up the Inside Passage to Dyea or Skagway, rough settlements at the very head of Lynn Canal, more than a thousand miles from Seattle.

For those in the first wave, in the early fall of 1897, there weren't even any docks to land at. Small barges, or lighters, came out to the waiting ships and everyone crowded aboard with their crates of supplies, tools, and food, everything they needed to survive. (To cross the boarder into Canada, where the gold fields were, you have to have supplies for a whole year, that worked out to about a ton). If they were lucky, they'd get ashore at high tide, cache their supplies in a big pile and walk around to get the lay of the land. If they were unlucky, they might arrive at low tide, have to trek their gear and food across a hundred yards of mud flats. And maybe after the first load, take a break, unaware of how far or fast the tide comes in, talk to others, have a look at town. And come back to find their gear and food underwater, maybe their dogs drowned: welcome to Alaska!

Top: Part of the fleet at Lake Bennett, ready to head to the Yukon. AM
Opposite lower left: The "Golden Staircase" on Chilkoot Pass. UW
Opposite right: One of the many Yukon River Rapids. UW

ISLANDER

"Them days it was every man for hisself. **The faster a boat could get out of (Skagway), the faster it could get back to Seattle or Vancouver and pick up another load of suckers.**"*

The towns they found on the shore, Skagway and Dyea, were full of card sharks, saloons, easy women, and a dozen other ways for the men to spend their money before they hit the trail.

Once they started out of town, on the trail to the "diggings," they had two choices: White Pass or Chilkoot Pass. Both were grueling slogs with heavy packs, taking trip after trip to bring the required ton of supplies to be allowed into Canada.

One of the powerful images of the Gold Rush was the long line of men trudging up the steep part of Chilkoot Pass. It was said that if you stepped out of line to rest, it might be a half hour before another opening in the line might appear for you to step into. For the wealthier there were native porters to carry your gear for pay. By 1898, there was an aerial tram to carry gear. But for the first wave of men of modest means, there was only that long slog, time after time, up and down, one foot after the other.

Next was the long downhill hike to the shores of Lake Bennett, where a little tent city was coming into being, for the lake was frozen, and the lake and the frozen Yukon beyond were the only way to get to the diggings.

There wasn't much sitting around - trees had to be cut, sawed into boards in the torture chambers called pit saws (One man on the top of the log, another on the bottom, pulling and pushing on the saw).

When the ice finally melted they launched the boats, some **5,000 (!!)** of them. Ahead were treacherous rapids and 500 miles of river.

And finally, perhaps 8 months after leaving their homes, they arrived at Dawson and the legendary Klondike River gold diggings.

Only to discover that all the claims had been taken, a bitter disappointment. Most men found work for someone else, made a little money and moved on into Alaska, where there were reports of other gold discoveries.

Of the 30,000 or so who actually made it all the way to Dawson, only a handful "struck it rich." Yet their adventure transcends time. All experienced the powerful drama of The North: the bitter cold, the wild characters, the incredible landscapes. Those who returned, even penniless, brought back stories to entertain generations of breathless children and grandchildren.

An early September afternoon, 1973. I am a commercial salmon fisherman, just my wife and I on our little 32' fish boat. We have four days off between fishing periods in Chilkat Inlet, near Haines. Together with a dozen or so other boats, all friends, we steam up to Skagway for the weekend.

Our group might be 25 total. But when the Skagway locals see us steaming into the harbor the word goes out: "Customers; gotta' stay open longer." And so the few restaurants and shops of this town of 800 stayed open for our little group, competing for our modest business.

It's not like that anymore, when a busy day might mean 10,000 visitors!

Revenue for the railroad in those days depended totally on a Canadian mine that shipped its ore by rail to the port at Skagway, to be put on ships that took the ore to a smelter in Tacoma. Back then the busiest days in Skagway were the twice weekly arrivals of the Alaska state ferry with a few hundred passengers. The railroad even closed down in 1982, when ore prices dropped.

Then along came the Alaska cruise industry, a few small ships at first, quickly growing into a whole new economy for Southeast Alaska. For Skagway it meant that the railroad would reopen and transform itself, with classic freight cars barged in from all over the country, refurbished and put back to use hauling cruise ship passengers, into the most popular shore excursion in all of Alaska.

Of course, when a town of 800 has to accommodate 10,000 visitors a day for most of the summer, along with the seasonal workers to support them, things, like housing especially, get stretched pretty thin. If you walk around town, you'll notice a lot of campers, tents, and old schoolbusses used for housing, making for a pretty fun social scene for all the young workers.

Top: Old Number 73, the one remaining steam engine, gets ready to pull another trip up to the Pass, Fraser Meadows and back. Big "73" is being rebuilt in 2018, but will be in service again in 2019.

Those gaunt-faced men have moved on to whatever fate The North had in store for them. But the town remains, historically important and looking much as it did then, when some 80 saloons and many professional women served the lonely men on their way north.

Skagway was essentially built between 1897 and 1900. It was the weather that kept the turn of the 20th century buildings intact. Buildings that would have rotted away without maintenance in rainy Ketchikan, endured longer in this much drier, sunnier climate.

Today, Skagway offers a unique experience to visitors. Even the vegetation and climate is different from the rest of Southeast Alaska because the town is under the influence of the harsher temperature extremes of the interior instead of the milder, wetter, maritime climate elsewhere in the region.

Skagway can get very busy. It is a not-to-be-missed town, but if you are a repeat passenger and are ready for something a little quieter, a fast ferry (45 minutes, $68 round-trip) can take you to **Haines** and historic **Port Chilkoot**, where there are some pleasant walks, a few galleries, and restaurants overlooking Lynn Canal.

Onto The Ice:

If You Haven't Been Up, better go!

A bove and behind Juneau, Skagway, Petersburg, and other Alaska towns are the vast flowing fields of ice that eventually end up as icebergs and smaller bits of ice in the mainland fiords like Tracy Arm and Glacier Bay itself.

Going in a chopper is an eye opening geology lesson. On this particular excursion out of Skagway, we flew a few miles south over Lynn Canal, then east and up a canyon, higher and higher until there were snow fields underneath, with here and there side canyons bringing in yet more snow. Then in a particularly dramatic moment, we swooped over a ridge and the land fell away to reveal a true river of ice, obviously flowing slowly downhill, the solid ice shattering into cracks and crevasses where it had to turn corners.

But it was also obvious that in the recent past the glacier had been much larger and higher. For eighty or ninety feet above the ice's surface was a "trim line" - where trees were still growing - showing where the ice had been sixty or seventy years earlier.

Above: a small crevasse on the top of the glacier. Where we landed, the crevasses were all generally small. The danger comes in winter, when snow covers crevasses, some large enough to swallow the unlucky. Some of the bigger ones can be fifty or sixty feet deep.

Right: look for the dark area on the hills on either side of this glacier: this is the trim line: where the beginning of the forest marks the previous height of the ice.

Mile 955 - Point Retreat Lighthouse - *named by Vancouver after armed natives repulsed his effort to land.*

Mile 975 - Icy Strait - *also named by Capt. Vancouver who was barely able to get his ships through in 1794, it was so choked with ice.*

Hawk Inlet *lies to the east here, location of the Greens Creek Mine, which enables workers to live in Juneau and commute to good paying jobs by fast ferry from Auke Bay.*

Top: small bergs, Le Conte Bay, 2013. Ice like this and even larger bergs were common throughout Icy Strait when I was there in 1965. In just those 50 some years since, the ice front has moved far enough up Glacier Bay that little ice actually escapes the bay anymore.

Above: fish buying scow, Inian Cove, 1965 - note the A&P logo - in those days the big grocery chain owned salmon canneries and boats in Alaska.

August, 1965: I am 19, engineer on a big Alaska fishing boat, anchored in Inian Cove, about 50 miles southwest of the entrance to Glacier Bay. It is a popular spot for the big seiners that work Icy Strait in August seeking out silver salmon.

A noise wakes me deep in the night. I sit up, feel it this time: something bumping into us. I think perhaps our anchor has dragged in the current, or maybe another boat in the anchorage has, allowing them to drift down on us.

I pull on pants and a sweatshirt, step out on deck in the chilly black. But it's something very different from what I had expected. Not a boat at all, but rather an iceberg had drifted into the bay and was moving slowly along our port side.

I gasp in surprise; it was my first season in Alaska and I had never seen an iceberg before. This one was probably 15' above the water, its top even with our top deck

The full moon had filled the berg with an eerie translucent light. I could see some gravel, lodged inside the berg, probably scraped off a valley miles away, decades before I was born. I reached out to scrape some off, but it was inside the ice and my hand just slipped off.

Then the moon went behind a cloud, the iceberg moved away in the current, and that magic moment was over.

Another August night, 1965: finished with my engine room chores, I get a cup of coffee and walk forward to our pilothouse to take my wheel watch.

Old Mick, my friend and the first mate, has bad eyes, the cook doesn't steer, the deckhand can't be trusted and the skipper likes his sleep. So much of the steering in the black falls to me.

The skipper shows me the line on the chart that is our projected route, and retires to his stateroom. Then Mick comes up for a bit, and we look at the chart in the dim red light. It's an old one, marked with notations like: "Bear on the beach, Aug 12, 1961," and Mick's rough fingers tap on one of the bays east of us.

"Angoon.. Indian village. Went in there in '31 on the old *Dora R.* Black, snowing like hell, nothing but compass and chart, no one had fathometers (depth meters) in them days. We went in slow bell, tooting that horn, and listening for the echoes off the rocks on either side.. That's how we did it back then.."

After a bit he shuffled off to bed and I was alone. I sat up in that big chair as the wheel moved back and forth with the autopilot. Now and again I'd look at the radar, the chart, make sure we were on course, record it in the log.

We'd made the turn into lonely Chatham Strait by then, and it loomed ahead of us, mysterious and dark. I found a faint rock n'roll station on the old AM radio, and just sat back.

Life was grand, grand, grand!

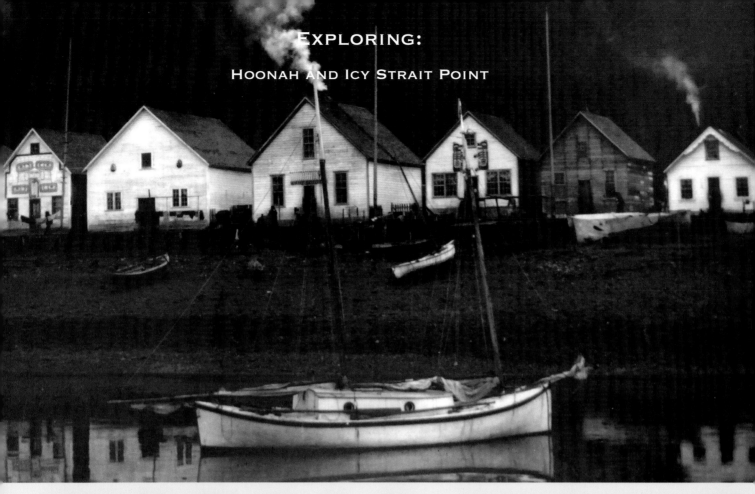

Top and left: early photos around Hoonah.

Opposite top: A zip line rider with Icy Strait Point (the old Hoonah Packing Company cannery) below. This particular zip has six parallel lines and is the longest ride of any zip line in Alaska. The ride ends at a restaurant, so you can catch a bite as well.

Opposite left: There is a pleasant short walk through the rain forest between the Cannery and the Landing Zone Bar and Grill. Easy wide path, definitely worth doing!

A CANNERY TURNED INTO A VISITOR ATTRACTION..
WHAT WOULD THE OLD-TIMERS HAVE SAID?

When it opened in 2003, Icy Strait Point was unique among Alaska cruise ports: ship visits are limited to one at a time, and the facility—a renovated cannery next to a Tlingit Indian village—is surrounded by wilderness. If you've cruised Alaska before, you know how congested the other towns can be with four or five ships in port at once. A visit here is a welcome change.

Passengers come ashore by lighter. The main feature is the cannery dock, which has a museum, cafe/restaurant, and numerous shops. Cannery life was a major cultural and economic element in coastal Alaska, and this is an excellent chance to get a close look. There are walking trails and a shuttle bus to nearby Hoonah, the largest Tlingit village in Alaska. The facility is owned by a Native corporation, which has preserved the rich Tlingit culture throughout.

Icy Strait Point is located in Port Frederick, just across Icy Strait from the entrance to Glacier Bay, west of **Mile 1080** .

EXPLORING:

JOHN MUIR AND GLACIER BAY

Imagine you're John Muir, an amateur geologist, in 1879. You're sure Yosemite's valleys were carved by ice, but no one believes you. You've heard a rumor that there were glaciers in faraway Alaska, so you take the steamer to Wrangell, hire some native paddlers in a big cedar canoe. You ask them to take you to the bay of big ice, but no one is really sure where it is except somewhere to the north.

And so in mid-October, Muir and his paddlers set out, crossing rough channels, sleeping in Indian villages. Arriving at the entrance, they

found a band of seal hunters from the village of Hoonah, persuaded one to come as a guide. The guide frightened Muir's paddlers with tales of friends who had drowned when icebergs came up from underwater and capsized their canoes. But Muir charmed them into continuing on and so entered Glacier Bay at last, which had emerged from the ice within the lifetime of his guide. He was stunned by what he found and immediately knew that what he saw confirmed his Yosemite theories, which were then reluctantly accepted by geologists.

Muir's discovery and what he wrote about it drew the first real tourists to Alaska, passengers on the big steamship *Queen* and others. They would go right up to the face of the mighty Muir Glacier which in those days was calving 10-15 big bergs an hour!!! Not only that but they would land passengers ashore and put up ladders to the top of the glacier face so that passengers could climb up and walk around!

Top: above Muir Glacier, 1893. American Geographical Society.
Above: Muir in Tlingit canoe, on his way to Glacier Bay. Christine Cox
Right: Glacier Bay today.

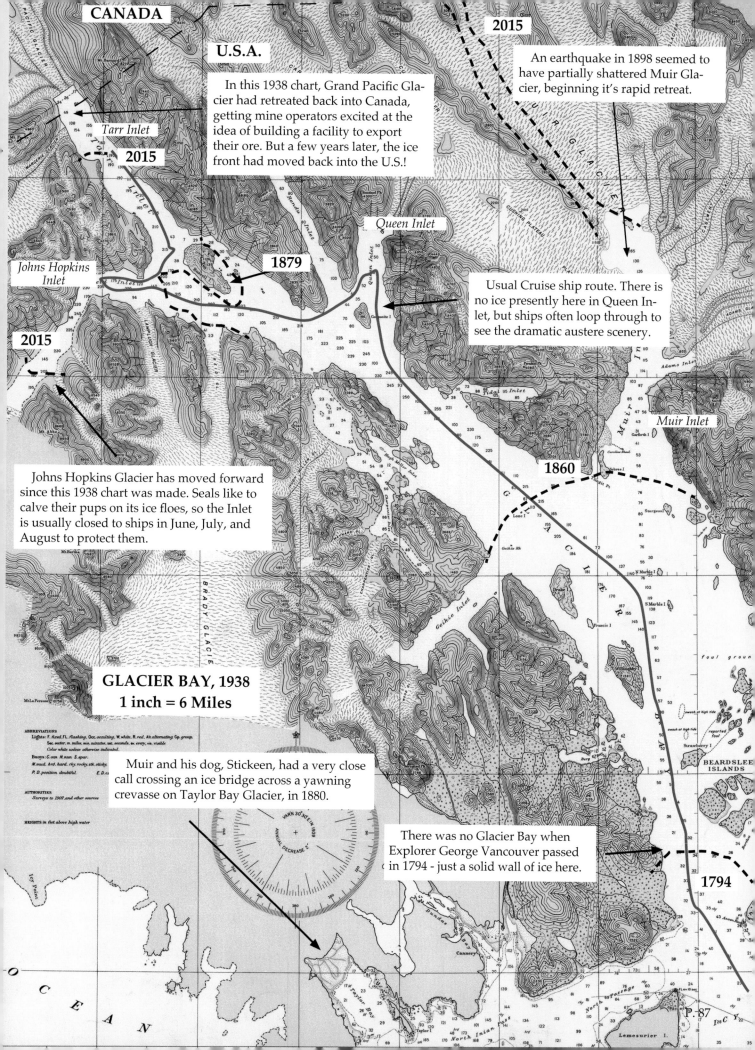

CANADA

U.S.A.

2015

An earthquake in 1898 seemed to have partially shattered Muir Glacier, beginning it's rapid retreat.

In this 1938 chart, Grand Pacific Glacier had retreated back into Canada, getting mine operators excited at the idea of building a facility to export their ore. But a few years later, the ice front had moved back into the U.S.!

Tarr Inlet

2015

Queen Inlet

Johns Hopkins Inlet

1879

Usual Cruise ship route. There is no ice presently here in Queen Inlet, but ships often loop through to see the dramatic austere scenery.

2015

Muir Inlet

1860

Johns Hopkins Glacier has moved forward since this 1938 chart was made. Seals like to calve their pups on its ice floes, so the Inlet is usually closed to ships in June, July, and August to protect them.

GLACIER BAY, 1938
1 inch = 6 Miles

ABBREVIATIONS
Lights: F. fixed. FL. flashing. Occ.occulting. W. white. R.red. Alt.alternating. Gp.group.
Sec.sector. m.miles. min.minutes. sec.seconds. ev.every. vis.visible
Color white unless otherwise indicated.
Buoys: C.can. N.nun. S.spar.
M.mud. hrd.hard. rky.rocky. stk.sticky.
P.D.position doubtful.   E.D.es...

AUTHORITIES
Surveys to 1907 and other sources

HEIGHTS in feet above high water

Muir and his dog, Stickeen, had a very close call crossing an ice bridge across a yawning crevasse on Taylor Bay Glacier, in 1880.

There was no Glacier Bay when Explorer George Vancouver passed in 1794 - just a solid wall of ice here.

1794

BEARDSLEE ISLANDS

KAYAKERS, LAMPUGH GLACIER:
WOULD YOU CAMP HERE?

When your ship enters lower Glacier Bay at about **Mile 1005**, you could be excused for asking, "So, where's the ice?" Well, in the 250 or so years (just the blink of an eye in geologic time) since the first white men saw the bay, most of the ice has disappeared and you'll have to travel almost 50 miles to get to the ice front.

The first ships always went to Muir Glacier, with a front around 200 feet high calving off **big** bergs at the rate of about 10 or 15 an hour! Today consider yourself lucky if you see one major calving event. Also before there were so many cruise ships in the Bay that the Park Service had to institute rules, ships would blast their big air horns which would sometimes dislodge enough ice for a dramatic photo. Today a cruise ship that did that might get fined or even banned.

Top: the front wall of a glacier is unstable, as the fresh ice fall in the pix shows. Probably not a good idea to camp too close.

Right: an apartment-sized spire topples into the water.

Above: probably 50 years ago, this glacier in John's Hopkins Inlet reached down into the water.

GLACIER BAY WILDLIFE

Top: Brown bear claws mussels off the rocks. Keep your binoculars handy. Bears are likely to appear on the hillsides above the bay as moving dots, as they gather berries. If the tide is low, you may see them along the shore as well. *Ki Whorton*

Left: For reasons not fully understood, Glacier Bay is also an excellent place for whale-watching. If you are exceptionally lucky you may see a breach like this one. *Minden Pictures*

Left, bottom: Seals are commonly seen on ice floes throughout Glacier Bay. So many use the ice calving from John Hopkins Glacier to birth their young that the Inlet is closed during the summer. If your ship goes in there, consider yourself lucky, as it is one of the most dramatic areas in the whole Bay.

Below: appearing like moving white dots on hillsides, you'll see mountain goats on incredibly steep slopes.

TRAPPED ON A GLACIER

L ook for tide rips northwest of the Inian Islands, near **Mile 1,026** as billions of gallons of water rush through constricted **North Inian Pass.** The three-mile-wide indentation to the north at **Mile 1,029** is **Taylor Bay**, leading to Brady Glacier at its head. Glaciologist extraordinaire John Muir was here in the summer after his 1879 Glacier Bay trip, hiking with a dog over the flats and up onto Brady Glacier on a cold and rainy August day. In the late afternoon, on his way back off the glacier, he had to take a running jump across a very wide crevasse, followed reluctantly by his dog, Stickeen. Fortunately the other side of the crevasse was slightly lower, but even so he had barely made it. A few minutes later he realized that he and Stickeen had jumped onto a sort of ice island, surrounded by wide and deep crevasses on all sides.

He found that the only possible two ways out were jumping uphill across the crevasse they'd jumped across downhill earlier, or across a frighteningly precarious ice bridge: curved, drooping, knife edged, eight feet down in a wide crevasse that fell away into darkness.

Muir chose the ice bridge, notching steps into the side of the crevasse, climbing down, straddling the ice bridge, and chipping away the sharp top edge into a narrow path that he and the dog could use to get across. As he worked, the dog whimpered and cried, staying back on the edge of the crevasse, refusing to follow.

Only with difficulty did Muir himself get across. It began to get dark, and finally he could wait for Stickeen no longer. He started to walk away, calling over to Stickeen that he could make it if he only tried.

"Finally, in despair, he hushed his cries, slid his little feet slowly down into my footsteps out on the big sliver, walked slowly and cautiously along the sliver as if holding his breath, while the snow was flying and the wind was moaning and threatening to blow him off. When he arrived at the foot of the slope below me, I was kneeling on the brink, ready to assist him in case he was unable to reach the top. He looked up along the row of notched steps I had made, as if fixing them in his mind, then with a nervous spring he whizzed up and passed me out onto the level ice and ran and cried, and rolled about fairly hysterical in the sudden revulsion from the depths of despair to triumphant joy. I tried to catch him and tell him how good and brave he was, but he would not be caught. He ran round and round, swirling like autumn leaves in an eddy, lay down and rolled head over heels."

- John Muir, *Travels in Alaska.*

Top: one of the vast ice fields that surround and create the glaciers in Glacier Bay. It was on one of these that Muir found himself and his dog trapped.

Above: artist's drawing of the ice bridge that Muir made his way across. Christine Cox drawing

The sea and landscape gets wilder and rougher as you transit **North Inian Pass** at **Mile 1,026** as the powerful winds, big seas and swells of the Gulf of Alaska (actually the North Pacific Ocean) make themselves felt.

This is Cross Sound where the ebbing currents from Icy Strait to the east and Lisianski Inlet to the south can make for confused and dangerous seas.

And it was near here that my friend Dave Kennedy bought a small fishing lodge for his retirement years after operating fishing boats on the east coast, the Gulf of Mexico, and out of Kodiak Alaska.

In Kodiak he was a pioneering shrimp fisherman, sometimes taking big chances, as many fishermen find themselves forced to do, trying to support a family and big boat payments. But his luck stayed with him, and he eventually left that hard life to the mellower waters and life of a fishing lodge operator.

But the sea is always waiting. For the unprepared, for the imprudent, or simply for the unlucky.

And one November, Dave set out alone in his outboard skiff for the morning bite in Cross Sound, hoping to get a nice big king for supper.

And never came back.

Mile 1,000 - Point Adolphus, *opposite the entrance to Glacier Bay, is regularly frequented by humpback whales. I was here in 1997 on the* Dawn Princess *when a group of four humpbacks appeared so close to the boat that you could smell their breath when they came back up from five or ten minutes underwater, and it was bad, bad, bad!*

Mile 1,027 - *road-less* **Elfin Cove** *has several sport-fishing lodges and a fish buyer.*

Right: Joe and Muz Ibach, homesteaders on **Lemesurier Island,** **Mile 1020** *spent their summers in a cabin on the spit at Reid Inlet, Glacier Bay, prospecting for gold.* Bradford Washburn photo.

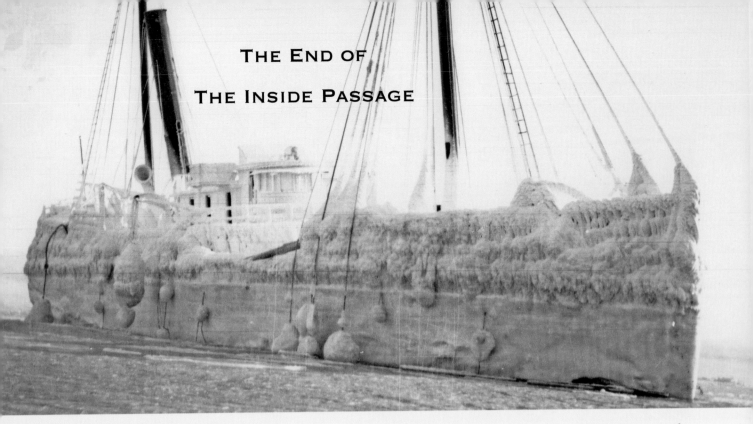

THE END OF
THE INSIDE PASSAGE

Cape Spencer, the lighthouse to the north at **Mile 1036** marks the end of the sheltered waters of the Inside Passage. Gone are plentiful harbors with easy access. To the north is the outside coast: bold, rugged, with few harbors and backed by the stunning and rugged St. Elias mountain range. Take the time to go on deck with your binoculars. In North America, only Alaska has a coast like this.

If the coast of British Columbia had been like this, the development of coastal Alaska would have been very different. The myriad harbors and sheltered passages of the Inside Passage allowed very small craft to travel to Alaska. Many would have never have headed north if their only route was outside along a coast like this.

Mariners sometimes stop their boat in the lee of the land here, check things in the engine room, make sure everything is tied down on deck, that there's nothing loose in the cabin that might break loose and hurt somebody. And make sure that everyone on board knows where their survival suits are.

These suits were invented by Seattlite Gunnar Guddal in the late 1960s, but acceptance by northwest fishermen came slowly until the Coast Guard required them on commercial vessels in 1991.

One of the first ever used in an emergency was about 20 miles north of the Cape, when a young man catching a ride south on a fishing boat grabbed one as the boat went ashore on a stormy night. Dawn found him alone on the beach, surrounded by pieces of the boat, but alive in his suit, the only survivor. Suits were new then and not yet in wide use among fishermen, so the suit's maker held a little press conference to give the man another suit. But the survivor said he wouldn't be needing it, that he was never going to sea again!

For boats traveling north in winter, icing up becomes a problem when cold wind blowing down off the mainland mountains and glaciers kicks up spray that freezes quickly on the boat's hull, making it dangerously top heavy and susceptible to capsizing. Sometimes the best thing to do in these situations is to head downwind, away from the land, sending crew out with hammers and baseball bats to get rid of the dangerous weight.

Top: iced up ship on the lonely coast north of Cape Spencer.
Left: Halloween costumes? No, the crew on my Bristol Bay salmon gillnetter break out their survival suits to lubricate the zippers and make sure they can put them on quickly in an emergency.

TERROR IN LITUYA BAY, MILE 1080

A round 10 on the evening of Aug 9,1958, anchored fisherman Howard Ulrich was awakened by his boat rolling suddenly in what had been a peaceful anchorage. He stepped up into the pilothouse and what he saw became etched into his mind forever:

"These great snow-capped giants (the mountains at the head of the bay) shook and twisted and heaved. They seemed to be suffering unbearable internal tortures. Have you ever see a 15,000-foot mountain twist and shake and dance?

At last, as if to rid themselves of their torment, the mountains spewed heavy clouds of snow and rocks into the air and threw huge avalanches down their groaning sides.

During all this I was literally petrified, rooted to the deck. It was not fright but a kind of stunned amazement. I do not believe I thought of it as something that was going to affect me.

This frozen immobility must have lasted for two minutes or longer. Then it came to a dramatic end. It so happened that I was looking over the shoulder of Cenotaph Island toward the head of the bay, when a mighty seismic disturbance exploded and there was a deafening crash.

I saw a gigantic wall of water, 1,800' high, erupt against the west mountain. I saw it lash against the island, which rises to a height of 320 feet above sea level, and cut a 50-foot-wide swath through the trees of its center. Then I saw it backlash against the eastern shore, sweeping away the timber to a height of more than 500 feet.

Finally, I saw a 50-foot wave come out of this churning turmoil and move along the eastern shore directly toward me."
— Courtesy of Alaska Magazine

This was an earthquake that knocked the needle off the seismograph at the University of Washington, 1000+ miles away. Ulrich and his son were lucky - their boat survived, barely. Another boat, the *Badger*, sank after being carried over the trees of the north spit. Its crew survived in a dingy but a third boat was lost with all aboard.

Ever since 1958, mariners anchoring in Lituya Bay do so uneasily. Wondering as they look up at the big glaciers behind the Bay: can it happen again?

Tidal wave from landslide stripped hillside of trees down to bare rock, to a height of 1,800 feet above the water!

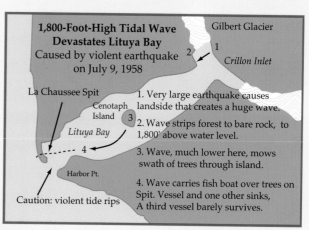

1,800-Foot-High Tidal Wave Devastates Lituya Bay
Caused by violent earthquake on July 9, 1958

Gilbert Glacier

Crillon Inlet

La Chaussee Spit

Cenotaph Island

Lituya Bay

Harbor Pt.

Caution: violent tide rips

1. Very large earthquake causes landside that creates a huge wave.

2. Wave strips forest to bare rock, to 1,800' above water level.

3. Wave, much lower here, mows swath of trees through island.

4. Wave carries fish boat over trees on Spit. Vessel and one other sinks, A third vessel barely survives.

Some itineraries to Sitka and south travel along the outside coasts of Yakobi, Chichagof, and Kruzof Islands. This is a remote and wild coast with hardly any settlements at all except Sitka itself.

Most passages along here occur at night; if you see any lights, they would most likely be from anchored fish boats. A few highlights along the way:

Mile 865 W - Lisianski Strait - *Winding shortcut narrow passage for small craft back to Cross Sound*

Mile 855 W - *Somewhere along this coast in 1794 Russian explorer Alexi Cherikof sent 11 men ashore in a longboat to explore. 4 days passed but they never returned, so he sent 4 more men in his other longboat. They did not return either, and Cherikof had to leave without them. No sign of them was ever found.*

Mile 815 W - Mt. Edgecumbe - *This dormant volcano was the first sign of land big lumber ships from Japan would see on their way across the Pacific to the Sitka Mill. It's also the site of a great April Fool's gag when a local jokester took a chopper full of old tires to the top, set them on fire, and passed the word around town: "She's gonna blow!"*

Top: a bad place to go ashore: rough seas on the outside coast.

Right: somewhere in the woods, an old blower waits for miners who will never return.

A COMMERCIAL SALMON TROLLER'S DAY

Commercial salmon trollers tow arrays of lures and baits, trailing back from weighted, mini winch operated 'downlines.' At any one time as many as 20 individual 'spreads' might be in the water behind the boat. When a fish hits, its struggles ring a bell on the pole, indicating which of the four downlines the fish is on. The troller winches up the down line, unclipping the 'spreads' and letting them trail behind the boat until he or she comes to the spread with the fish. Sometimes a fish that is fighting particularly aggressively will be sent down again to wear it out, rather than risk losing it. Once gaffed and landed, it is cleaned and either iced in the hold or on 'freezer boats,' frozen and glazed. Freezer equipped boats can stay out for weeks at a time, while ice boats deliver every few days.

Typically a troller is worked by two people, and fish for king salmon and the more abundant, but less valuable silvers.

When I was a troller in the early 1970s, fishing the rough waters off of **Noyes Island, Mile 720 W** a really good day was 15 kings, usually at least 20 pounds each. Two decades later, due to the success of salmon hatchery programs, 100 kings a day was not uncommon! Today, due to a warming and more acidic ocean, catches are declining.

Right: a 'smiley' or big king. Dan Kowalski photo

Mile 725 W - Helm Point, *a bold cliff, rising almost a thousand feet, is the most dramatic headland in SE Alaska.*

Mile 700 W - Cape Addington *is a long point sticking far out into the wind and seas, a particularly challenging spot for smaller trollers that frequent these waters in the spring. I was here in my 32 footer in 1973, and sometimes I had to screw my courage on pretty tight to put in a day out there.*

Mile 680 W - *A few miles to the east here is* **Waterfall Resort**, *once one of the biggest canneries on the coast. Today the small worker's cabins have been converted to guest suites.*

Mile 660 W - Forrester Island *is today a wildlife preserve, home to thousands of seabirds. Years ago, when small trollers fished here, a enterprising gal set up a bakery in a tent.*

Peril Strait is a winding shortcut between Sitka, on the outside coast, and the more protected inner waters of Chatham Strait. Here the tide runs strongly enough to suck the big Coast Guard navigational buoys completely underwater.

The Alaska ferry *LeConte* hit a rock here in 2004 and almost sank. It was Sitka's main ship connection to the 'outside' and was out of service for much of the season. Electronic glitch with the navigation equipment? Nope, human error...

Top: western part of Peril Strait from about 25,000 feet. Rock ferry hit is near the two islands beneath aircraft wing.

Below: ferry LeConte in Peril Strait in better days, near the exact spot where she was to become impaled on a rock a few years later.

Once it was cannery workers that filled the long row of south facing waterfront houses. Then the cannery closed, and it became more of a summer and weekend community for folks flying out from Juneau.

Fortunately, in 2015, at least, there were still enough students for the State to fund a teacher, and thereby allowing families with children to stay, a critical component of small town life.

The tidy covered hot spring in the center of town makes the long winter go a lot easier.

An active fleet of commercial salmon trollers operates out of Tenakee.

Top: **Rosie's Blue Moon Cafe** *was a lot busier when the cannery was running and the loggers were in town. But sometimes it was got rough: "They alla time wanna fight," said Rosie.*

Upper left: Alaska kids are tough; this was the last week of May, and they were swimming. Not dipping... swimming.

Upper right: unloading the Alaska Seaplane Beaver. The load that day was frozen goods for the store, a tire for a four wheeler, a big solar panel, and mail consisting of a sack of letters and about 20 Amazon boxes.

WHERE RUSSIA BECAME AMERICA

Consider yourself lucky if your ship stops here. The lack of a dedicated cruise ship dock (some ships tie up at a facility 5 miles from town with shuttle buses for passengers) and a location slightly off the beaten path make for a more mellow downtown than Ketchikan, Juneau, or Skagway.

Sitka was the capital when Alaska was part of Russia from the late 1700s until 1867. With brutal efficiency, sometimes slaughtering whole native villages if they didn't hunt for them, the Russians forced natives to hunt and kill sea otters for their valuable fur. Those furs created an empire that stretched from the Aleutians all the way down to Northern California.

Those were good years when Sitka was the busiest port on the Northwest Coast. Its residents drank fine wines and enjoyed ballet, at a time when Ketchikan and Juneau were native villages.

After the Russians slaughtered the sea otters almost to extinction, and Moscow was humiliated by Britain and France in the Crimean war in the 1850s, Russia was almost broke, and approached the US about selling Alaska. It was a great deal for the US: $7.2 million, about 2 cents an acre, and was completed in 1867.

However the purchase was ridiculed as Seward's Folly or Seward's Icebox (William Seward being the Secretary of State at the time). Critics were silenced when gold was discovered.

After the Americans took over, Sitka slowly evolved into a sleepy fishing and logging town on the ocean side of Baranof Island.

In more modern times, Sitka's economy depended on the big plywood mill out in Sawmill Cove, and on commercial fishing. The closure of the mill in 1992 was a major financial blow to the town. But instead of languishing, Sitka experienced a slow renaissance based on the arts and, to a lesser degree, tourism.

Today, having missed the booms and busts of the gold rush, Sitka has become the cultural center of SE Alaska.

Top: view to the south from Castle Hill.
Right: salmon gillnet crews - Sitka is a major commercial fishing center.

Top: snowy owl at Raptor Center, where injured owls, eagles, and hawks are cared for after being injured. Those that heal completely are often released into the wild. Those with injuries that prevent them from flying again are often sent to zoos or other wildlife centers, while others live on at the center.

Left: new and old totems at the Sitka National Historical Park, a short walk to the east along the shore from where passengers come ashore from ships.

Far left: a young cookie vendor - with many fewer visitors, the retail scene in Sitka is much mellower than in either Juneau, Skagway, or Ketchikan.

Mile 1045 - *Fish buying vessels often anchor in the few protected bays just north of Cape Spencer. They offer, fuel, water, ice and limited groceries to their boats. And if a boat is really lucky, maybe a hot shower or a load of laundry.*

Mile 1075 - *The narrow entrance to Lituya Bay is particularly dangerous when the tide is ebbing against the usual southwest wind. French Explorer LaPerouse lost 21 men here in 1786, when their longboats were swept into the tide tip. If your ship passes close here, use your binoculars; you might see wrecks of fish boats.*

Hermit Jim Huscoft lived on Cenotaph Island in Lituya Bay for years. A boat would drop off supplies once a year.

Mile 1105 - *Caution: breakers have been observed as much a two miles from shore off* **Dry Bay.** *All the rivers along this part of the coast have shallow entrances often swept by breakers, and should be attempted only with local knowledge.*

However, there was a good run of salmon into the Situk River in Dry Bay, and a cannery in Yakutat that wanted the fish, but the entrance was too dangerous. Soooo.. they built a 60 mile long railroad!

Top: Dawn Princess off **Cape Saint Elias, Mile 1310,** *a major landmark along this coast.*
Right: La Perouse Glacier.

L ook for **La Perouse Glacier, Mile 1060**. With its almost perpendicular 200- to 300-foot face, it's an outstanding landmark along this section of coast. This is an active glacier. As recently as 1997, it was advancing into the ocean, after having receded far enough to allow foot passage across the face at low tide. It's one of the few glaciers in Alaska that fronts the on open ocean and not on a protected bay.

This is probably the least visited part of Glacier Bay National Park. Occasionally hikers or even mountain bikers have flown in with their gear, landed on a sandy patch of beach and started hiking. It was always an arduous task here: inflating tiny rafts to ford cheeks, pushing heavily loaded bikes over boulder strewn beaches.

To the east is mostly wilderness, a vast region from the coast up over the Fairweather Range and into Canada's Yukon Territory almost to the Alaska Highway.

East and north of Hubbard Glacier is an area that has been nicknamed "The Roof of North America"—an immense rock, ice, and snow world with many of the continent's highest peaks. Ten thousand-footers are common here, and there are at least four higher than 15,000'.

Much of this area is the Wrangell-St. Elias National Park and Wilderness. This mountain wall catches the wet, eastward-flowing air, creating heavy snow. The immense weight of the snow pack creates the largest glaciers on the entire Pacific coast, part of a vast ice mass that extends parallel to the coast in an unbroken line, except for two places, almost 400 miles to Anchorage.

Something woke me deep in the night, and I sat up in my bunk suddenly, listening. The engine of our king crab boat was just idling long - that was odd; but it was something else that had woken me. Then the boat took a sudden roll and I felt it; our motion was slow and loggy, very unlike the quick roll she'd had when I went to sleep. Up in the pilothouse I saw the problem as soon as I looked out the window: ice. Though we were five miles from land, the bitter wind flowing down the Copper River valley had chilled every part of our boat so that the spray flung up by the sea had become a thick layer of ice, making our boat dangerously top heavy. We didn't have to be told what to do: we knew that if we didn't beat off the ice and shovel it over the side quick, we would capsize before morning.

Without a word, we suited up in hooded snowmobile suits. Another crewman and I inched out onto the bow, where the 2" diameter pipe rails around the bow had become so thick, they were growing together into a solid wall of ice. With baseball bats and hammers we broke ice off the rails and anchor winch, kicking the pieces over the side. Once the bow dipped deep into a big sea, and we were instantly waist deep in swirling water that pulled at us before suddenly clearing away as the bow rose again.

Only after two long hours did the boat seem to ride a little higher, roll a little quicker. But we knew that if the wind picked up even more, it would make ice faster than we could knock it off and we'd have to turn around, and run downwind out into the ocean, away from the bitter land breeze.

"It's the Copper River Wind, boy," the mate told me. "All that air just gets frozen up there and rolls straight down the valley to the ocean."

ICY BAY HIGH SCHOOL

A few years back I got an Icy Bay High School graduation card from a friend's son. It had a school logo and certainly looked like the real deal. But then I got to thinking: the only things in Icy Bay were a small fishing lodge, and a logging camp that I thought was closed up.. No way were there enough kids for a high school...

A little later I bumped into my friend and asked her about her son and the card.

"There isn't any high school," said she, "Our son is the caretaker of the logging camp, they're the only family there. They're homeschooling the kids. They just thought he should have a graduation card like the real ones so they printed one up."

---

*Hubbard Glacier lies at the head of Yakutat Bay, **Mile 1165**. It is only occasionally visited by cruise ships, usually those which have been unable to get a permit to visit Glacier Bay.*

***Malaspina Glacier, Mile 1200**, is about the size of the state of Rhode Island.*

*When Captain Cook passed **Mile 1210** in 1776, he found a tongue of ice sticking several miles out into the ocean. Since then, the ice has retreated back into **Icy Bay**, though small bergs still make it out into the open ocean.*

Top and below: our king crabber, the Flood Tide, *iced up off the abandoned settlement of Katalla.*

Mile 1250 - Cape Yakataga - There used to be a camp here for crews drilling exploratory wells for oil. Once a fishing boat had shipwrecked a few miles away and the oil roughnecks were startled at lunchtime with the crew of the fishing boat staggered into their mess hall wearing only rubber boots and bloody long underwear!

Mile 1310 Cape St. Elias - look for the dramatic 500' tall pinnacle rock just offshore from the lighthouse. Your author almost lost his life here when the crab boat he was on iced up. (See previous page.)

Mile 1350 - Copper River Delta is the site of the salmon gillnet fishery that produces the well known Copper River Reds, popular as the first fresh salmon of the year.

Mile 1380 - Cape Hinchinbrook, entrance to Prince William Sound.

Top: Harvard Glacier, at the head of College Fjord

Right: The Exxon Valdez *was dodging ice when it hit a well marked reef on a calm March evening in 1983, spilling some 11 million gallons of heavy crude oil.*

It was a major blow to commercial salmon fishermen as the oil moved west, closing commercial fishing areas as it passed. It took over 25 years to settle the lawsuits! As the expression went: "The only ones who win are the lawyers."

The hidden jewel of Prince William Sound is remote **College Fjord**. Within an eight-mile stretch at the upper end of this fjord five major tidewater glaciers reach the salt water. While Glacier Bay has emerged from the ice so recently that substantial trees have not gained foothold close to the ice, College Fjord is a place where the forests and glaciers have coexisted for centuries.

The result is a perspective on the great rivers of ice not seen in Glacier Bay. To see a glacier towering above the 100-foot-tall trees of a spruce forest, like Wellesley Glacier is really impressive.

Study the hillsides here. The upper slopes of these big glacial fjords, stripped of trees and covered with many berry bushes, are excellent bear watching territory. What you are looking for are brown or black dots that appear to be moving—these will be bears foraging for berries. Look also for white dots, often found in small groups—these will be mountain goats. You will see goats in places that an experienced rock climber would probably have trouble on.

Bears are also found down on the beach, especially if the tide is low. They are pretty good clammers, despite a crude technique. It goes like this: they look for the telltale water spurts of clams, dig them up with a big paw, smash them open with their other paw, and press the whole mass, shells and all, up to their mouth.

So where are the really big icebergs? By the time most of this ice gets to the salt water, it has been fractured so much by those twisting mountain valleys, that most of the ice that breaks off is fairly small, say the size of a two car garage at most.

Exploring: Chiswell Islands,

Kenai Fjords National Park

Into the Great Sea Cave

Once I was a guest lecturer/naturalist aboard this small (100 passenger) cruise ship and we stopped at the Chiswell Islands, part of the Alaska Maritime Wildlife Refuge, west of Seward.

Mildred was a sprightly lady, whose family had brought from a nursing home in Maine, to be with them on this trip. 90 years old or not, she wanted to go on every adventure, every excursion.

But on the day we visited the Chiswells, there was a big swell running, making it awkward, borderline dangerous, for us to get aboard the big Zodiac inflatables for the excursion. I tried to point out the danger, but Mildred was having none of it, and so the Filipino crew waited for the right moment, grabbed her, and plunked her safely aboard.

When we got close to the islands, the big swell was just booming into the sea caves, throwing spray far and wide.

"C'mon, Joe," Mildred said, "Take us into the sea cave."

"Mildred," said I, "That'd be too dangerous; we'd be smooshed.."

"I know," said she, "but that's so much better than wasting away in the nursing home..."

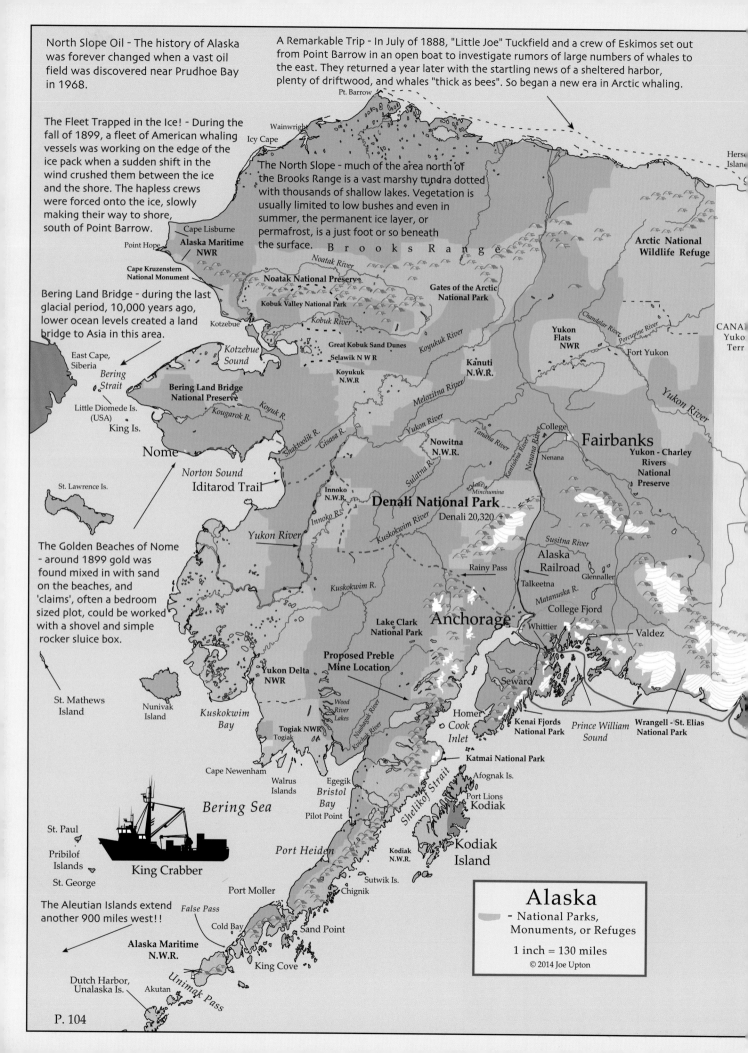

North Slope Oil - The history of Alaska was forever changed when a vast oil field was discovered near Prudhoe Bay in 1968.

A Remarkable Trip - In July of 1888, "Little Joe" Tuckfield and a crew of Eskimos set out from Point Barrow in an open boat to investigate rumors of large numbers of whales to the east. They returned a year later with the startling news of a sheltered harbor, plenty of driftwood, and whales "thick as bees". So began a new era in Arctic whaling.

The Fleet Trapped in the Ice! - During the fall of 1899, a fleet of American whaling vessels was working on the edge of the ice pack when a sudden shift in the wind crushed them between the ice and the shore. The hapless crews were forced onto the ice, slowly making their way to shore, south of Point Barrow.

The North Slope - much of the area north of the Brooks Range is a vast marshy tundra dotted with thousands of shallow lakes. Vegetation is usually limited to low bushes and even in summer, the permanent ice layer, or permafrost, is a just foot or so beneath the surface.

Bering Land Bridge - during the last glacial period, 10,000 years ago, lower ocean levels created a land bridge to Asia in this area.

The Golden Beaches of Nome - around 1899 gold was found mixed in with sand on the beaches, and 'claims', often a bedroom sized plot, could be worked with a shovel and simple rocker sluice box.

The Aleutian Islands extend another 900 miles west!!

Map Labels

Pt. Barrow
Wainwright
Icy Cape
Cape Lisburne
Point Hope
Alaska Maritime NWR
Cape Kruzenstern National Monument
B r o o k s   R a n g e
Noatak River
Noatak National Preserve
Kobuk Valley National Park
Gates of the Arctic National Park
Arctic National Wildlife Refuge
Chandalar River
Porcupine River
CANA Yuko Terr
Herse Island

East Cape, Siberia
Bering Strait
Little Diomede Is. (USA)
King Is.
Kotzebue
Kotzebue Sound
Kobuk River
Great Kobuk Sand Dunes
Selawik N W R
Koyukuk River
Koyukuk N.W.R.
Kanuti N.W.R.
Yukon Flats NWR
Fort Yukon
Yukon River

Bering Land Bridge National Preserve
Koyuk R.
Kougarok R.
Shaktoolik R.
Gisasa R.
Melozitna River
Yukon River
College
Fairbanks

Nome
St. Lawrence Is.
Nowitna N.W.R.
Tanana River
Kantishna River
Nenana River
Nenana
Yukon - Charley Rivers National Preserve

Iditarod Trail
Norton Sound
Innoko N.W.R.
Innoko R.
Lake Minchumina
Denali National Park
Denali 20,320 +

Yukon River
Kuskokwim River
Sulatna R.
Susitna River
Alaska Railroad
Rainy Pass
Talkeetna
Glennaller
College Fjord

St. Mathews Island
Nunivak Island
Kuskokwim Bay
Kuskokwim R.
Lake Clark National Park
Proposed Preble Mine Location
Anchorage
Whittier
Valdez

Yukon Delta NWR
Wood River Lakes
Nushagak River
Koichak River
Seward
Homer
Cook Inlet
Kenai Fjords National Park
Prince William Sound
Wrangell - St. Elias National Park

Togiak NWR
Togiak
Walrus Islands
Cape Newenham
Egegik
Bristol Bay
Pilot Point
Katmai National Park
Afognak Is.
Port Lions
Kodiak
Shelikof Strait

St. Paul
Pribilof Islands
St. George
Bering Sea
Port Heiden
Kodiak N.W.R.
Sutwik Is.
Chignik
Kodiak Island

King Crabber

Port Moller
False Pass
Cold Bay
Sand Point
King Cove
Alaska Maritime N.W.R.
Dutch Harbor, Unalaska Is.
Akutan
Unimak Pass

Legend

Alaska

 - National Parks, Monuments, or Refuges

1 inch = 130 miles

© 2014 Joe Upton

THE VASTNESS:
WESTERN ALASKA

Western Alaska is mostly road less. Travel is by plane, boat, snowmobile, and even dog sled occasionally. The invention of the snowmobile around 1960 transformed winter transportation in much of The North. Before snowmobiles, many Natives in remote areas had to keep large teams of dogs, catch and dry fish to feed them, and take care of them for the rest of the year in order to have them for winter travel.

The land is dotted with tiny Native communities. Life is often a struggle with income from seasonal construction jobs and fishing often not enough to last through the long winter.

A very large part of this land is tundra—wide areas of spongy wetland dotted by shallow ponds. In the darkness of the long winters, all this land sleeps. But the Arctic spring begins an awakening process that transforms The North.

The great flyways bring millions of migrating birds to the vast delta country of the Yukon, Kuskokwim, and smaller rivers. The long days cause vegetation of all sorts to grow at a rate not seen elsewhere.

Top: Aniachak Volcano with its steam vent looms over the Ugashik River. Many of these volcanoes are active. When I was a king crab fisherman working on the Bering Sea after dark, sometimes an eruption would fill the sky, seen just by us crab fishermen, and a few hundred natives.

Before the arrival of modern social services and the cash economy, winters in the far north could be another word for starvation if game was scarce.

In those days, the sea and land provided a hard living. The result was a remarkably tough and resilient people. In boats made of walrus hides stitched together and stretched over driftwood frames, they traveled hundreds of miles to hunt bowhead and other whales. Other hunters waited for hours by holes in the ice for a seal to surface briefly to breathe.

Housing was sod and earth huts, or igloos in winter, and skin tents when families moved to be closer to fish runs in the summer. When the white men came, Eskimos quickly learned about commerce and the value of their ivory carvings. As soon as the gold rush created settlements of whites in western Alaska, Eskimos began to camp nearby to carve and sell ivory.

Today's Eskimos are more apt to live in prefab houses delivered by barge and depend on seasonal fishing and construction work.

Above: "Summer Camp," a painting by Ken Lisbourne, Point Hope. Often Eskimos, especially those living near the deltas of the great Yukon and Kuskokwim rivers, would travel to campsites on the water where they could catch salmon and set up drying racks. In addition to preserving fish for themselves, they would often dry many chum salmon to feed their dog teams over the winter. Author's collection

Right: Yu'pik Ircit, or human/fox mask, from the author's collection. Eskimo legend has it that Ircit were extraordinary persons who appeared alternately as humans or small mammals. This would be revealed as footprints that would alternate between animal and human tracks.

Opposite page, top: "Shoppers" aboard a trading schooner, circa 1920. Each year, trading vessels would travel north to Bering Sea Eskimo villages loaded with supplies such as sewing machines, five-gallon tins of kerosene, Aladdin Lamps, fabric, rifles, and all manner of smaller items. Natives like these women would come aboard with skins or ivory to trade for supplies. UW17962

Opposite page, bottom: Ivory Carvers during the Nome Gold Rush. UW17963

EFFECTS OF A CHANGING CLIMATE

It's completely beyond what any of our models had predicted."

"I never expected it to melt this fast."

Such were the comments from scientists at a recent symposium on the Arctic. There still may be debate in a few quarters about global warming, but not in Alaska—it's here.

The tidewater glaciers on the Alaska coast had been receding slowly for decades, even before global warming became a household word. But recent events in the Arctic and their implications for the future are sobering, especially for species dependent on wide areas of sea ice such as the polar bear.

Until a decade or so ago, sea ice covered most of the Arctic Ocean in winter, melting and receding a bit in the summer, and then refreezing quickly again each fall. But recently the sea ice has receded dramatically in the summer. From 1979 to 2000, the average area of ice in the Arctic Ocean was around three million square miles. By August of 2007, that number had shrunk by half, a truly staggering reduction. One scientist predicted that the Arctic would be ice free in summer by 2030.

It may happen sooner. As ice melts, the darker ocean absorbs much more heat than the white ice which reflects the sun's rays, further increasing the melting.

The climate change will create losers and winners. The Northwest Passage shipping route from Atlantic to Pacific would become reality. New areas would be open for mineral and oil exploration. Valuable fish species such as salmon and pollock might thrive by moving their range farther north. The polar bear would probably be a loser, depending on the ice pack for habitat.

Many Native villages in the Arctic are built close to the shore, but had been protected from storm seas by a natural barrier created by the ice. As the ice recedes, the seas become larger, and villages may either have to relocate or eventually be swept away. Permafrost–frozen earth close to the surface of the ground is another huge issue. Most small buildings and houses in the Arctic essentially have permafrost foundations. As the ice in soil melts, the buildings slowly settle into the soggy ground.

Can global warming be stopped? In theory, perhaps. But the realities of a rapidly developing Asia and a global economy built on high energy use make it unlikely.

So, if you want to see Alaska in its present state, go soon

Alaskastock Photo

Joe and Matthew Upton
Katmai, AK, 1997

Traveling northwest waters as a commercial fisherman for 20 years, Joe Upton gained intimate knowledge of the coast from Puget Sound to the Bering Sea.

In the 1970s Upton lived and fished out of a tiny island community in the roadless wilderness of Southeast Alaska. His first book, *Alaska Blues*, based on those years, was an instant classic.

In 1995 Upton established Coastal Publishing to share with the new travelers to Alaska some of the drama he had seen in his travels, producing illustrated maps and *The Alaska Cruise Handbook*.

In 2010 Upton teamed up with filmmaker Dan Kowalski to produce unique mini documentary films that can be accessed at www.alaskacruise-handbook.com.

Upton lives with his wife on Bainbridge Is, WA, and Vinalhaven Island, ME.

ALASKA

ALASKA PENINSULA AND

1915 Map prepared by whaling company, showing their ship routes as well as gold deposits, etc. Note that Anchorage was so small in 1915 - just a few tents on the beach - that it didn't even make it to the map!

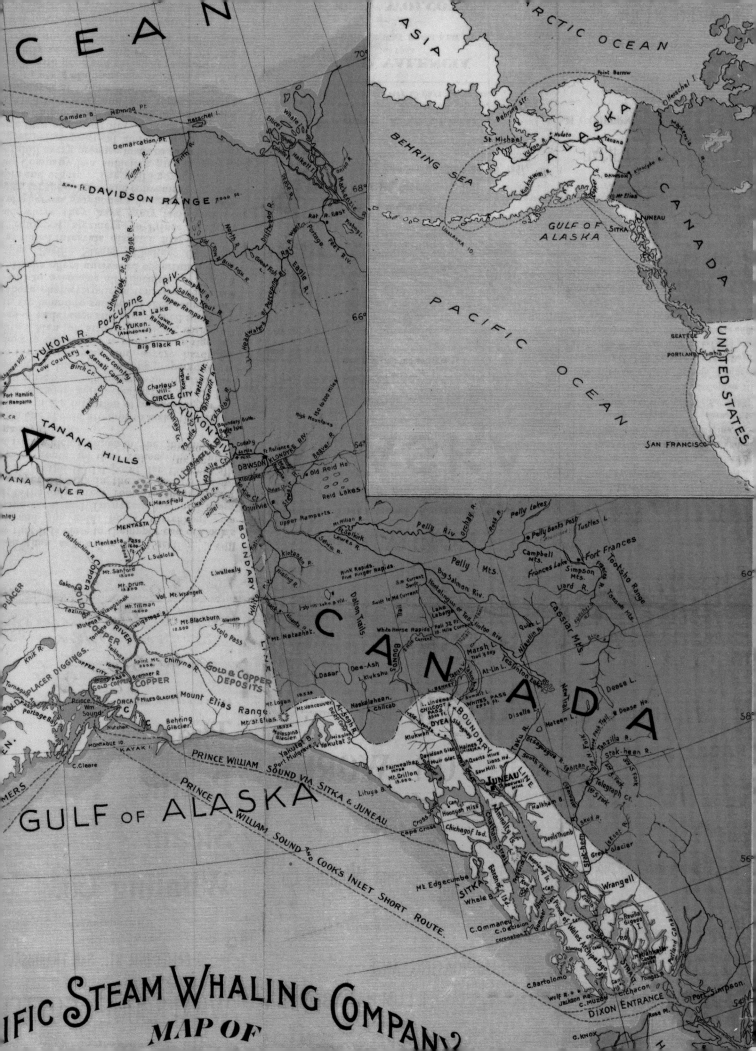

This 1918 Post Office route map shows the challenges of getting the mail around western Alaska. The winter routes are by dog sled, and the summer routes by steamboat or horseback. This map is one of many at: www.historicalcharts.noaa.gov.